Souls of the Asylum

Souls of the Asylum

A Clairaudient Experience

As received by
Doug and Berta Lockhart

BALBOA
PRESS
A DIVISION OF HAY HOUSE

Copyright © 2013 Doug and Berta Lockhart.

All rights reserved. No part of this book may be used or reproduced by any means, graphic, electronic, or mechanical, including photocopying, recording, taping or by any information storage retrieval system without the written permission of the publisher except in the case of brief quotations embodied in critical articles and reviews.

Balboa Press books may be ordered through booksellers or by contacting:

Balboa Press
A Division of Hay House
1663 Liberty Drive
Bloomington, IN 47403
www.balboapress.com
1-(877) 407-4847

Because of the dynamic nature of the Internet, any web addresses or links contained in this book may have changed since publication and may no longer be valid. The views expressed in this work are solely those of the author and do not necessarily reflect the views of the publisher, and the publisher hereby disclaims any responsibility for them.

The author of this book does not dispense medical advice or prescribe the use of any technique as a form of treatment for physical, emotional, or medical problems without the advice of a physician, either directly or indirectly. The intent of the author is only to offer information of a general nature to help you in your quest for emotional and spiritual well-being. In the event you use any of the information in this book for yourself, which is your constitutional right, the author and the publisher assume no responsibility for your actions.

Any people depicted in stock imagery provided by Thinkstock are models, and such images are being used for illustrative purposes only.
Certain stock imagery © Thinkstock.

Printed in the United States of America.

ISBN: 978-1-4525-7183-6 (sc)
ISBN: 978-1-4525-7185-0 (hc)
ISBN: 978-1-4525-7184-3 (e)

Library of Congress Control Number: 2013909299

Balboa Press rev. date: 7/8/2013

Book Dedication

This book is dedicated to all that are touched by its message; to all those that receive its message and are able to step back and acknowledge a much larger picture.

Thank you goes out to all of the group members that are in the physical realms now for their tireless work and dedication to see that the awareness is made for the conditions of the cemeteries.

Also to the countless meetings and negotiations to see that the headstones be placed and common dignity restored.

Thank you to the group members in the energetic or spiritual realms that encourage and move about to aid the universe in the direction of positive response and for their patience.

A thank you to the mothers of both Berta and Doug for their passing on of their abilities that allow them to see, hear and move things that are present yet unseen to the eye. Thank you for allowing the movement to continue within them.

Thank you to all others for the aid and participation whether great or small for the support or the research and for the many hours it takes to put together a work of this kind.

With all of this said, and from the greatest depths of our hearts, we thank you, all of you and each of you.

Ted's Group

Epigraph Page

Athens Lunatic Asylum 1874-1993

"We are more than just a number –remember us for we, too, have lived, loved and laughed."

Table of Contents

About the Receiver:　　　　　　　　　　Ted's Group

Foreword:　　　　　　　　　　　Sharon K. Grossman

Chapter 1:	Slim Hardgrove	1
Chapter 2:	Red	5
Chapter 3:	Sarah Jensen (Swather)	25
Chapter 4:	Riley	27
Chapter 5:	Mary (Margaret) Schilling	31
Chapter 6:	Raymond	35
Chapter 7:	Etta Gabriel	39
Chapter 8:	Emily Jarvis	49
Chapter 9:	Josiah Whipkey	51
Chapter 10:	Martin (Marty)	55
Chapter 11:	Emma Holsinger	59
Chapter 12:	Joseph Enochs	65
Chapter 13:	Mrs. Elizabeth Walker	69
Chapter 14:	Mary Chaney	73

Chapter 15:	Mary Sprouse	81
Chapter 16:	John Doe – "Eddie" David Edward Littmar	85
Chapter 17:	Eliza Fe la Quois Smith	91
Chapter 18:	Dr. Samuel D. Wallace	99
Chapter 19:	Adaline Hall	107
Chapter 20:	Mahala Butler	113
Chapter 21:	Hampton Dixon	119
Chapter 22:	Eliza Gerhart	129
Chapter 23:	Elza F. Stevens	141
Chapter 24:	Charles Warrick	145
Chapter 25:	Mathias Cook	151
Chapter 26:	Simon Archer	157
Chapter 27:	William Buchanan	161
Chapter 28:	Red	169
OFFICIAL NAMES OF THE ATHENS LUNATIC ASYLUM		173

List of Illustrations

vii	Photo by Danielle F. Russell
xxvi	Photo by Danielle F. Russell
xxix	Photo by Brigette O'Rourke
xxxii	Photo by Danielle F. Russell
4	Photo by Danielle F. Russell
7	Photo by Danielle F. Russell
16	Photo by Bryan David DeLae
18	Photo by Brigette O'Rourke
23	Photo by Bryan David DeLae
24	Photo by Tom Miller
30	Photo by Tom Miller
33	Photo by Tom Miller
38	Photo by Tom Miller
43	Photo by Danielle F. Russell
44	Photo by Bryan David DeLae
50	Photo by Danielle F. Russell
58	Photo by Danielle F. Russell

64	Photo by Danielle F. Russell
68	Photo by Danielle F. Russell
72	Photo by Danielle F. Russell
80	Photo by Danielle F. Russell
84	Photo by Danielle F. Russell
90	Photo by Danielle F. Russell
94	Photo by Danielle F. Russell
98	Photo by Danielle F. Russell
105	Photo by Brigette O'Rourke
106	Photo by Danielle F. Russell
112	Photo by Danielle F. Russell
118	Photo by Danielle F. Russell
124	Photo by Brigette O'Rourke
128	Photo by Danielle F. Russell
140	Photo by Danielle F. Russell
144	Photo by Danielle F. Russell
150	Photo by Danielle F. Russell
156	Photo by Danielle F. Russell
160	Photo by Danielle F. Russell
166	Photo by Danielle F. Russell
168	Photo by Danielle F. Russell
Authors	Photo by Reyna Garcia

About the receiver:

Doug Lockhart was born in 1963 in a small rural town of Maryland. His first few years came to be for the most part uneventful with an early childhood development, but at the age of nine his world seemed to stop and take a completely different direction with the announcement of his parents' divorce. In the early 70s divorce was still a dirty word not easily mentioned in any crowd and carried with it an amount of shame and embarrassment. Since nobody in his immediate surroundings experienced this, it left him vulnerable and alone.

Stepping back into the earlier days, Doug was exposed to various aspects of the unexplained as his mother dabbled in different areas of the paranormal arts; the Ouija board, channeling, automatic writing, ESP, spoon-bending, the misunderstood development of the power of the mind, self-healing and palm readings. Many of these activities were taboo even in those days and were often kept secret or shared only within a select group. His exposure to these was very limited due in part to his age, but mainly as they dealt with adult levels of understanding. His mother dabbled mostly alone, and learned as she could from the limited authors that were available at that time.

Early memories created fear and misunderstanding within him; when Doug was about six years old, he happened to peek down the stairs when it was presumed that all of the children were asleep only to view his parents in the middle of a séance. At the age of six, he witnessed four adults sitting in chairs flat-footed and all hands upon the surface of a card table as the table was elevated above the floor. Even at this age, he knew that this was contrary to all laws of order. It created an early childhood fear and closed doors for him for many years to follow. His mother continued to channel and wrote as he grew, but since Doug was closed to this early on, any information presented was quickly disregarded and mentally filed away as hogwash.

Years passed without any real involvement in any spiritual work at all, he barely made it through school, as he was academically poor in most subjects. He was average at math skills as long as they contained numbers and not theories. English, Writing and Reading were of no interest at all and very difficult for him. History was an interest as long as it was American History, as all other eras seemed too long ago to be concerned with. When he moved into the arts, that is where he found his strength, comfort and solace. Anything that had to do with shapes, perspective, illusions or capturing a moment in time with colors, basically any form of art that meant using his hands, intrigued him.

At the age of 14, he began working with a local flame artist blowing glass. He proved to be competent and efficient as well. So much so, that ideas and techniques seemed to come out of nowhere, which helped him excel quickly in that field. At 16 years old, he started his own business and began traveling to various art festivals. He earned a reputation and received many awards for his work.

As a high school senior at 17, decisions regarding the direction of studies and college selections, as well as future plans were pending. He sought a school to teach glass blowing on a large scale, but none seemed suitable. He discovered a trade school in West Virginia that taught a program called "Heritage Arts," the study of 18th and 19th century trades and traditions. This seemed very interesting and his application was mailed and accepted. Many hand course studies were taken; spinning, weaving, log home construction, furniture making, basket making, and blacksmithing. The day he walked into his first blacksmith shop he saw an amazing transformation that felt all too familiar to him. As a glass blower, he watched as hard glass heated to a molten state could be manipulated and transformed to something far more grand and majestic than that of its original state and once allowed to cool down remained in that state.

The very same amazing transformation was taking place before him now as cold hard steel was heated then manipulated through the use of hand tools to something so grand and magnificent from its beginnings, that it left him breathless. The only difference between the two mediums was that once cooled, the metal object was not prone to break and in many cases could last forever. It was at that moment that Doug knew in his inner core that he was meant to be an ornamental blacksmith. One often knows the unforgettable feeling when touching upon the gift that you possess and are meant to pursue, whether it is music, arts, healing, service or one of the many other gifts one possesses.

In 1981, he picked up his first hammer and his work and style began. Once again recognition and awards for his work came as he never settled for average work to come from his hands. His intrigue and wonder moved him above those around him quickly. While seeking his look or style, he realized that his interest in metal work was vast and although his style was established, his focus could not be contained and he often found himself in many different areas of metal work. He took a series of part-time jobs in order to survive after leaving school with a two-year program.

He married in 1987 and began to fulfill another lifelong dream of marriage and family. Two years later, he found himself empty and not quite knowing what was missing. He began to sense the emptiness was spiritual in nature. He didn't understand the emptiness or its origin since he was not raised with it. Why would he feel it was missing from his life now? He lived within walking distance of a small Mennonite church in Ohio and felt it was the church to visit. It was there that a teaching of God the Father, Jesus His Son and the Holy Spirit was taught and accepted. He accepted the teachings wholly and made his life correspond to this new understanding without any previous exposure.

Doug accepted this teaching as a young believer without years of debating the word of God, and applied it literally to his life. He found himself moving more and more toward a conservative way of life as he grew in his spiritual knowledge. Hard work was no stranger to him and he often found himself doing whatever he could to provide for his family. He raised produce, raised draft horses, logged timber with horses, worked carpentry jobs, and shoed horses; all the while continuing to produce blacksmith work.

It is interesting to note that Doug is a true artist. You will rarely find him comfortable in any setting where the conversation turns to him. He prefers to stay toward the outer edges of the spotlight. He has given credit to a source other than himself on more than one occasion for the inspiration and actual completion of something produced with his own hands. He often stepped back with his mouth agape staring at the wonders of the work he had just completed. When asked, "How did you come up with this concept?" he would simply state, "It wasn't me, I was merely a vehicle to complete this task, what you see is far greater than I am able to produce alone."

Soon Doug and his wife were given a daughter who became the focal point for all he knew, wanted and longed for. There was rarely a moment when his daughter would be out of his sight. He carried her in a backpack and the two of them were inseparable. When completing yard work, milking goats, cutting firewood, or cleaning stalls his daughter was either on his back or right at his side. Life was good, orderly, simple and moving in the direction he wanted.

Two years later they were given a son only to be taken again 3 days later due to complications at birth. This separation caused great depths of hurt and confusion within Doug and it rocked the very core of his foundation. Instead of happily rejoicing in the moment of the birth of a son he found himself digging a grave and making a small casket of cherry wood. He wondered the entire time what the lesson to be learned from this was. Where was God at that moment to allow such grief? It was his understanding that the event was the start of the downward spiral in the breakdown of his relationship with his wife. Moments of highs and lows abounded and as time went on more lows seemed to occur than did any highs. Through all of this another son was given and joy was in his heart once more.

Realizing what was of strict importance and the responsibility of two children was so dear to him. Life was confusing to him. He found such solace with his children yet he found such turmoil between his wife and himself.

Searching for his source of strength, comfort and answers led him back to his church, but answers did not seem to be available and more questions formed as the emptiness deep inside him expanded with each passing day. He struggled and although an amount of safety was present in his familiar comfort zone; externally with his relationship to his wife, but even more threatening was the turmoil inside, an internal battle and a pulling from left to right.

After 19 years of marriage and many attempts to repair shattered emotions an ending was made to the marriage and a new direction was firmly sought after. This decision meant that he would have to step down as a member of the Mennonite church, a Sunday school teacher and a Youth bible school instructor as well. Life at this time was overwhelming for sure, so much uncertainty, so much confusion and so many unanswered questions.

Months of living in a small cabin secluded and surrounded by woods and solitude provided many opportunities for reflection. The silence gave him the needed opportunity to seek what was right to help put events in order and to gain perspective on his life. Then a beautiful being walked unexpectedly into his life: a woman that had been a friend for many years, but only on the surface of a relationship. She offered him everything he was seeking: love, acceptance, support, and kindness. Among these she offered the smallest yet most important things to him. She looked at him as they shared; she wanted to go for walks in the woods and was elated at the presence of a sunset. Things that in many ways seem minute yet are in many ways monumental parts of a relationship; everything Doug longed for, everything he hoped for. A new purpose was established for him, a new direction to point in and a new hope of a future of joy, peace and happiness.

Realizing that an uncanny or unexplainable familiarity existed between them and after accepting the closeness described only in books or by other people existed, Doug and Berta were married in early 2009. Along with this union came another daughter 14 years old. Life was good again with a new purpose; love, three children and a healing. They attended and visited different churches and congregations as a family. Although the singing was good and the messages were received, they seemed to be left with an indescribable hunger and unfulfilled feeling that seemed to linger. Sure the closeness of gathering with neighbors and friends was there, but something else was desired and what exactly that was, was not known; perhaps a closer loving relationship with God and answers to questions of life and death and the general understanding of the offerings of the universe. What is our purpose and our origin? Are we destined for something and if so, what?

In late January, word came to Doug of the petition for a large art commission by the City of Athens, Ohio. The city was planning the construction of a roundabout and wanted to commission a local artist for the artwork at the center. Doug went to work designing and an idea popped into his head. A design that was unique, wonderful and meaningful all at the same time. This roundabout is located just across the Hocking River between Ohio University and the old hospital or Athens Lunatic Asylum, known today as "The Ridges." The asylum is not in view of the roundabout and Doug's concept was to take an aspect well known as a symbol of the asylum and make a collage of the cast iron window grilles. The beautifully intricate and ornate designs would be used to tie the two landmarks together, all the while creating awareness of the very historic landmark known as Athens Lunatic Asylum.

It seemed a good idea to drive the 40 minutes to the old asylum to photograph the different grille designs to help in the concept layouts. Upon arrival to the back of one of the dorm wings the weather was great, the sun was just right for photographing and Doug was snapping pictures one after another. The moment his wife Berta stepped from the car she started to feel sick to her stomach and politely waited for Doug to finish. They drove to the front of the asylum to photograph different design examples and Berta did not share her condition. They later realized that the main administration building was now an art museum and felt it was a good way to stretch and perhaps photograph the inside of the building, so Doug, Berta and their daughter ventured inside the art museum with all areas of artwork.

Doug and their daughter wandered ahead and Berta lagged behind feeling more and more nauseous with each step. Unusual feelings of heaviness, sadness, hopelessness and heartache combined into one made for quite an uneasy stomach. She didn't understand this overpowering feeling and yet didn't share this with Doug, not wanting to spoil the afternoon. While the others visited and explored, Berta stayed behind and sat alone on a bench still pondering the source of her overwhelming condition. They left the museum inspired, not as much by the art exhibits but more by the building and its architecture. Although she still did not feel well, Berta noticed that at the exact moment that they left the grounds, all of the symptoms she had been experiencing previously left her instantly. It left in such a way that it was as if a great weight was lifted or removed from her. It was such an incredible contrast that she then shared her experience with the others. Doug sensed this was strange.

It was then apparent to many here that due to the choices and paths voluntarily chosen by Doug that time was of the essence. Meaning that things needed to be encouraged or helped along. Blocks were in place and creating obstacles. A two-week honeymoon, if you will, took place after the union with his soul mate and then work needed to be done. That is when we woke him up!

At about 3:00 A.M. on March 1st, 2009 Doug was jolted awake by the sound of what he saw in his mind, meaning that the visual contrast was so loud that his sight was confused with sound. Regardless, the result is exactly what was intended. He saw a pitch-black background with the bold stark white letters spelling "WAKE UP" that gained his attention with a jolt. Once he gained his senses for a few moments the next word was "TED." In his mind he knew that the message meant wake up and pay attention to what I am about to tell you and that the individual speaking to him was named Ted. So as usual during inspired moments Doug reached for his sketchbook by the nightstand and began to write what he was hearing. He woke Berta and together they began this journey.

Crying, trembling and overwhelmed with emotion, he kept saying aloud, "I don't want to do this," yet he continued writing in a manner of necessity, rather than willingness. The first writings were interesting to observe because so much happened in a short time. We watched him deal with fear, doubt, uncertainty, release, intrigue, belief, skepticism, amazement, and unworthiness; emotions that ran the gamut. We watched as he and Berta worked through each and every one of them together. We watched them grow together and their flip of emotions. Skepticism turned to belief, fear turned into calmness and acceptance, uncertainty became dedication and unworthiness became knowledge and remembrance. It was quite a ride to say the least.

When he realized that he was in fact gifted to receive, he began to listen more intently and learned to delicately tune in his receiving in order to receive more easily and precisely. Meaning it became easier for him to hear the voice of his Guide and the vibrations created by the Ted's Group. Much effort went into the preparation of this work: the bringing together of two very powerful energies was important, for should an energy of this level exist, it makes transmitting and receiving very easy and exciting. A tremendous eagerness to do so exists. Introductions to teachings and the slow chipping away at the foundations of the walls that Doug willingly allowed to be built needed to take place. As his awakening occurred and the ability to work through the blocks was achieved, we were in fact able to transmit and he was able to receive and this work began to take shape.

As interesting and captivating as this work is, keep in mind that it is in fact only the beginning of what is to come. This work is only a springboard to the following. This awakening that we refer to is the knowing or remembering of what is to be and has been, meaning simply that Doug and Berta are in fact part of Ted's Group also. While on this side of the veil, they both agreed to return not only to receive this work and aid with the cemetery, but also to help create the awareness of the mistreatment of the socially insane, the value of the communicating ability, the receiving of vast amounts of knowledge, the understanding of the veil, heaven and the universe, the purpose of physical man, placement and the relationship of man and God, what happens when you leave your physical form and what is next. These are all things that you know in your inner self, but part of what is lost and forgotten when transition is made from nonphysical to physical and physical to nonphysical. Those questions can be answered and remembered, without jeopardizing the learning paths before you.

We are Ted's Group; a group of 177 nonphysical energies that have dedicated themselves to the restoration of the Athens Lunatic Asylum Cemeteries and to the stories of those that were part of this experience. There is also the physical part of Ted's Group; Doug, Berta and 108 energy souls that have agreed to, in a physical manner, do the physical part to see that it is accomplished. Working together this is an extensive work and an exciting understanding. It is important that you move on in your understanding and knowing after reading this book. It is our purpose that you do so, for there is much to know between the physical and nonphysical. There is forgotten information waiting for you just beyond the veil. Allow yourself to be open to the receiving and the life that you experience now will seem and become stagnant. An exciting journey awaits you as well, once you allow it; one of excitement, fulfillment, knowing, understanding, insight and the answers to many questions. All you need to do is remember. Our greetings to you from beyond the veil.

Ted's Group

Foreword

WHETHER YOU ARE INTO CHANNELED MESSAGES or not, you might agree that if ever a group of deceased people would desire to reach out to someone—anyone who would listen—to tell their stories and be understood, the Athens Asylum patients would be those people.

I first met Doug and Berta Lockhart under a canopy tent in the middle of the town square in Logan, Ohio, where I interviewed them for an article I was writing. They were selling hot dogs and other refreshments at a community concert to raise funds to buy memorial markers to place on numbered graves at the former Athens Asylum cemeteries in Athens, Ohio. It was one of those supposedly one-time meetings that ended up ballooning into a special relationship. I later joined the work of The Lockhart's and others on this cemetery project. Our mission: Give dignity back to the patients buried in these cemeteries by identifying each by name, birth date and death date.

The channeled stories in this book are from those patients. The stage was set many years ago, 1868 to be exact, when the Athens Lunatic Asylum was first built as a state-of-the-art institution for the treatment of PTSD of Civil War soldiers and other mental illnesses. It was one of several regional treatment centers, incorporating the then known methods of dealing with psychiatric disorders. Some physical ailments such as tuberculosis were also treated. The institution was discontinued in 1993 and ownership of all but the cemeteries were transferred to Ohio University.

Today, driving into the complex of the old asylum, now known as The Ridges, visitors immediately notice the beautiful architecture of the buildings, how the institution's grounds were laid out, and the new art museum housed in the main building. Yet an underlying, troublesome memory stream flows undetected to the uninformed eye. Until the visitor realizes that approximately 70,000 patients passed through the doors of these buildings during the entire time of its operation (which amounts to the total population of a city nearly the size of Wilmington, Delaware), they will miss the gamut of human experience which invisibly permeates its very atmosphere.

Each and every person who walked those tiled floors of the asylum was just like us with families, hopes and dreams, and memories of lives lived. Whether they were treated for a mental or physical illness, this asylum became their placeholder in society where they could be safe and hopefully sent back out free of that which admitted them there.

Some of those 70,000 patients did get better and went home. Some never left the site once the doors closed behind them. When over 1,700 of these died at the asylum and were never claimed by families, their bodies became forever attached to the history of this property in a macabre way. Buildings can be renovated and repurposed, but row after row of numbered graves forever marks this place as what it was in days gone by. For those left in these temporary burial plots never claimed, can we in good conscience ignore who they were, what they did, or diminish the worth of their lives because of their illness, the location of their final resting place, or the fact that all we can see are numbers on their graves? Amazingly, we have tolerated the dehumanization and archiving of these individuals in unmarked graves as mere examples in the name of historical preservation, to illustrate how procedures were carried out in the past.

This collection of channeled stories from beyond those anonymous graves will at times make the reader uncomfortable; bring tears, and even anger. You may not want to believe their tales or will dismiss the means by which they were received. But this is the vital human element of this historical site of a forgotten group of individuals who, if we could only hear, would cry, "We are more than just a number!" That element is the driving force behind preserving these stories in book form.

As one interested in the preservation and documentation of the whole of American History, I feel these channeled stories are an important addition to bricks and mortar, good intentions, numbers and statistics. The Lockharts found themselves thrust onto center stage of a drama that no one knew existed until now. I can attest to their integrity and love for those patients that chose them to share their stories and nominated them to help clear their unfinished business. Doug and Berta are compelled to share what was given to them. Holding back would be the real travesty.

Read these patient's stories. Never forget them.

Sharon K. Grossman
American History Examiner, Haunted Places Examiner
Examiner.com

Arlan Nitter
?–1877

Souls of the Asylum

Here you go again reaching for another book that has drawn you to its content and hoping that the questions within you will perhaps be answered this time. You are in many ways about to fulfill your desire. The work that is about to unfold within your hands is a preconceived work, a book that will entice you to believe in that which you are already aware of and that which is unseen. It is also a stepping-stone for works that are to follow. There are some books that have been produced that will leave you empty and continuing in your search. Absorb what you are about to experience and allow what you already know to be confirmed.

"*Souls of the Asylum*" is a collective work. There are in fact many authors and a receiver on your vibrational level was used to produce this work. It contains accounts by the people, the lure of the cemetery, the draw and wonder of the unknown, and perhaps the answers to mysteries of generations. It's the lure of the unmentionables that has attracted so many to this work. The taboo word "lunatic" and the idea of trying to understand more of the inner thoughts of a person labeled as such. The anticipation for answers to the lingering questions as to what really happened to the people buried in those graves and its great mystery will help provide closure.

A very large amount of common everyday people walked through the halls and stayed in the rooms at Athens Lunatic Asylum from 1874 through 1993. The asylum offered all it could to remove and house those deemed unacceptable from general society for reasons as varied as the spectrum of color. The majority were contained, few were helped and some remained. This is a small representation of life within and outside the asylum from those who experienced it. How are these accounts possible?

There are approximately 2018 graves in the three cemeteries located on the grounds of the asylum that are marked primarily with numbered stones. Some will never be marked. Approximately 1774 of these stones are in need of attention and 1695 are only marker stones. The marker stones have only the burial number upon them in order to identify the grave, without names or dates. All information about the individual below is in many ways lost to history.

The travesty is the fact that these people were born to parents, may have had siblings, may have grown and produced children, in some way made an impact on earth, were given a first and last name, may have had a pet growing up, may have been special to someone and touched their life, were given honor and created, lived through experiences that shaped their personality, saw things and held them and something touched them, more than most. Something so intense reached their core, the very place where light and energy are produced, and as a result they responded in a way to this event that was deemed inappropriate or unnatural and were met by disapproving souls around them.

This is the oldest of the three cemeteries at The Athens Lunatic Asylum in Athens, Ohio

That is how many ended up at the asylum for the insane. Not that Athens Lunatic Asylum is in any way different from asylums all over the world, because it is not, although it is the one place chosen for its story to be released. It was a sad and dark experience for them, given the fact that upon entering the front doors of the asylum, they no longer existed and if they were one of the unfortunate to pass over in the asylum and not be claimed by family, they were then awarded as property of the state and buried in the asylum cemetery. Once they finished their days there, they lost everything: their dignity, respect and history and were placed into a shallow grave and only marked with a number.

This is where we come in to the picture. There are approximately 177 energy souls that have in some way been in or at the asylum that have moved beyond the veil, the separation of our two existences, earth and heaven. The author chose to be the receiver of our stories while he was here in a past experience, a common man working as a blacksmith willing to hear and write for us. Just as each person speaks or communicates on earth in different pitches of vibrational transmissions, so it is on the other side. As stories were related to the receiver, each story was translated through one person, Ted, chosen for speed and clarity and thus this group became known as Ted's Group.

Are we lingering spirits stuck at the asylum? No. Are we hanging in limbo unable to move on? No. We have all chosen to stay or rather not to incarnate again and return until we accomplish our goal. We are all beyond the veil and chose not to move on to experience all the wondrous glories that are here until our goal is reached. A benefit of being here is that we are able to be there also, so we do move between here and there and do occasionally visit the asylum as well as many other destinations.

What are our goals and their parameters? Very simply, we have agreed to choose a small group of 27 to relay the accounts of their lives while on earth with the events leading up to and including their experience at the asylum. Collectively these stories told differently end up with similarities, seeking awareness of the cemeteries and the disrespect of the headstones. It is the intention of Ted's Group to shed light on these events through this awareness. We would like an additional stone placed below the existing stones and only the names and dates of birth and death to be added. In doing so a respectful end will be given to those who walked the very earth as you are. Perhaps awareness can be made of this same occurrence in other locations and a reckoning may be seen on a larger scale.

I speak as if I was at the asylum and in fact I was, and I too am part of Ted's Group. I am able to speak to you because of my release. If I were to represent myself as I was last before I left that existence, you would find great difficulty in understanding me. My story, although as valuable and interesting as those you are about to read, was not chosen for this work, but is in no way more or less important or interesting as any of those who are buried upon those grounds. Allow me to revisit my days for a moment to help you understand:

"Seeking to no my sole and to beleave in this that be false me, to no al

that is everything that is to hold to this worlb that makes me sad. I'm alone and afraied to no wy i ned this in mi days to live in this plase. Come to me and i wil leeve with thos thet wish for me to hold on to and stil wunt to walk with me. My stay is long and I wish fore my end to com todaye. Pleze do not talk to me just onle com to tek me."

You must understand that once I left that experience I left everything: feelings, thoughts, burdens, everything. I walk differently and relate differently and visit the experience only in memory, as do all that are here with me now.

We are all excited that you have found what you've needed. Through this work many doors will be opened to you and a growing of knowledge and understanding will take place. So open these pages and experience the lives of some of those that found themselves at the asylum. Feel them, get to know them and perhaps you, too, will remember. Help where you can, know what you feel and realize that your experience is only momentary, but it is in fact, unique and needed. Thank you and may you be truly enlightened.

Arlan Nitter
#12
1877

Chapter One

Hello. I am Slim. I was sent to the Athens Mental Hospital. I suffered from epilepsy. I developed this problem when I was 9 years old. I was not born with it. It was a mild case of epilepsy and although I did have seizures, they were not very frequent.

In many outward respects, I looked and often acted normally. My seizures were debilitating at times. They numbered from 6 to 9 per year. This was mild to many. I scared my parents as the information to them was limited and treatment was unknown. Epilepsy is difficult for everyone because it flares up without warning and you never see it coming. They had no idea how to treat its symptoms and the seizures were quite frightening to me as well as others afflicted by it.

I was aware of my seizures, but my body froze and convulsed in spasms. My throat and tongue stopped their normal activity. I could see, but not focus or move my eyes in any voluntary manner. I wanted to stop, but my body overrode my mind and desire. Usually my teeth clenched so tightly that I feared I would crack my teeth and it felt as if my jawbones would explode.

No treatment was offered to me. No special provisions were made and my work included many tasks. I was admitted to Athens Mental Hospital when I was 14 years old. I was from a farming family with a small farm in West Liberty, Ohio. I had many skills and was helpful.

I worked outside mostly and preferred it that way, as some really scary people were inside who were truly crazy. Those people drooled and peed on themselves and on the walls. They yelled for no reason and cried or talked to themselves. They dragged themselves when their legs did not work. They were sad and needed help. I preferred to stay outside and away as much as I could. I was good at picking up the yard, clearing and hauling brush. I worked on the laundry some and at the pump house where I would grease machinery.

I stayed at Athens for 9 years. My family thought I was retarded, since they were confused as to how I seemed to act like a normal young man in between seizures. What they saw was the fact that my episodes started at 1-3 per year and increased to as many as 8-10 per year. My family believed I would eventually be in a continual convulsive state, which was not the case.

Ray (Raymond) was a very large black man and next to my scrawny white 14-year-old frame, he appeared even larger. I was assigned to him in the yard. You will find no pictures of Ray, for while he was staff, no photos were taken of the darkies at Athens. He was a good man and he was a good teacher. He was hard and firm with me and we spent much time together. His job was to carry a small stick in his pocket to put in my mouth to keep me from cracking my teeth during a seizure. He was to sit on me until I stopped convulsing to keep me from hurting others or myself, but mostly myself. He was good at this and performed this duty for many years.

I left Athens when I was 23. I wanted to stay badly, for it became home to me and Ray was not only my close friend, but could read when seizures were about to start; he could just tell. The reasons given to me for my release were that the space at Athens was limited and although I had been a good help to the staff, I was still not staff and the bed I occupied during the night was needed by very ill people, unlike myself. I was sent to a hospital in Columbus and then sent to Youngstown Border, Pennsylvania. It was not a hospital, but a home for new drug treatment.

I liked Athens. I was never mistreated. The food was always terrible and cold, since retards and crazies did not care anyway. I was somewhat aware of the bad treatment of others at Athens, but I chose to stay out and away. There was nothing wrong with me; I simply had an imbalance in my brain. I later responded to drug therapy, although my convulsions never ended, but became less violent. I left the home and became independent. I got word of work in Pittsburg and found work with the Pennsylvania Rail Yards. I married and had no children, for fear of passing along epilepsy to them. I died at 69 due to smoking. Dumb, huh? My wife was Sylvia Hardgrove.

Slim Hardgrove

Chapter Two

I am William, known as "Red." I was missing front teeth. I was a staff member at Athens Lunatic Asylum. Everyone called me Red. I was average height. I was hired on as an orderly or staff of the patient rehabilitation team. I had no experience in any medical fields. My jobs were never outdoors, but indoors. I coordinated the daily handling of patients. I was taught to move, restrain, and hold patients to keep them from hurting themselves as well as others. I was provided housing at the hospital, but I later moved away. I saw and knew much. The asylum was not a good place. It was a prison with grass.

I hardly know where to start: doctors or nurses directed all of my experience with the mental patients. I only did what I was told. I was assigned to the men's wing mostly, but I, along with others, was involved unofficially in the women's wing. The directors only wanted male staff with men and female staff with women, but when the directors were gone, the female staff would always welcome the extra restraining help provided by the men (as you can imagine). The transfer always turned perverted and so much needless abuse took place. I feel I would like to tell some of the many things I knew.

The asylum was not intended to take mentally ill people, fix them and then help them get home to their loved ones and live normal lives. It was nothing more than a paid prison that would house socially undesirable people indefinitely, or as long as they continued to receive payment for doing so.

Many good people passed though Athens. Many were well intentioned, but peel away all the multitude of layers and you will see the real images. Doctors and nurses with good intentions came through trying to "cure" the insane. Many levels of insanity existed; mentally handicapped, physically deformed, criminally insane, substance abusers, emotionally damaged, retarded, and Mongoloids.

The asylum's existence was due to the fact that we could take what society neglected and place them out of sight. Much of all you know of the asylum is not accurate. Many pictures were taken of the asylum in order to travel to collect funds and direct interest into the complete well care of the mentally ill. Public and private funding resulted. You will find most of the people in some photos were staff, not patients.

It is true that the original intent of the asylum designer was to provide activities, work, homelike atmosphere, and social activities as a means of treatment, but let me ask this: if the home environment was what many of these people were removed from in the first place because they were not able to function, respond or behave, what made them think that reproducing it in a separate location would make them suddenly become whole? First attempts at taking different photos were a disaster, as we were unable to get any of the patients to sit still long enough for a photo. Very, very few patients ever dressed in the manner depicted in the pictures you will find of the asylum. Many wore gowns and minimal clothes. I saw very few people dress in that manner.

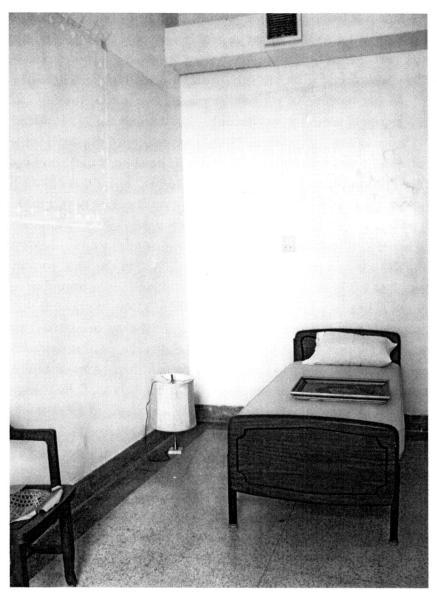

"...the original intent of the asylum designer was to provide activities, work and a homelike atmosphere"

Ideas are just that, ideas. Ideas of good intention were soon replaced by necessity. For example; in the early days of Athens Lunatic Asylum you found rooms for patients with beds, bookshelves, and decorations for comforts, but as people destroyed the surroundings and hurt themselves, these items were removed and not replaced. They were found to be just that, great ideas with ineffective results.

As the number of patients increased, one room housing and single patient rooming became one room housing with 2-4 patients with beds sometimes stacked. Patients were grouped by needs. Some were allowed to have rooms with beds and bedding, which consisted of a steel bed frame, a cotton stuffed bed mat, and a wool blanket (some had a small pillow), but the severe patients that were hard to handle occupied other rooms. They rarely wore clothes voluntarily. Whenever visitors came, we were alerted to take a box of gowns and did our best to tie them on. We tied them in the back, so they were less likely to be removed. Many of these people were foul or pitiful. They let go of any of their bodily functions without notice. Some sat in their waste or smeared it on themselves or others. This was bad enough, but some worse cases threw their shit at the walls and anyone in the way. These wards or halls housed more of this kind. Almost entire halls were void of any furniture at all. Beds were removed. A straw filled mat on the floor was provided for sleeping. These were removed often and burned as they became foul shortly. It just became easier for everyone; no clothes, no furniture, and all smooth surfaces to keep it sanitary.

Problems arose with staff, as it was their responsibility to keep the hall clean while on their shift. Many staff built up resentment, as I did. Often thoughts were shared amongst staff and violence would occur. Nobody liked to clean up shit or piss all day and we had limited means to do so. Many times we felt isolated, as we were not allowed out either. Food was brought to us. We never took these patients outside or provided activities. We watched insane people cry, scream, sit, shit, lay and behave in manners that were completely or often opposite of what was accepted by all humans.

Staff became resentful and inwardly angry. I included myself in this group. Compassion lasted only for a short time and was soon replaced with thoughts of just killing them because they were not right. Staff performed many beatings. I remember beating many with a leather strap because of the inconvenience and unpleasantness of the tasks that I had to perform each day at work. I remember thinking, "if you would be normal and shit like a normal person, I wouldn't have to clean you up and the floor." My anger came out in different ways. Since I was inconvenienced and my work was mostly unpleasant, I felt it necessary to pass along my feelings of unpleasantness. I beat them so they felt bad and in turn, I felt better. Often I hit a patient that did not respond with the cries I was expecting and that would make me feel angrier, so I beat them even harder.

We used buckets of water to throw on the patients in order to clean them because we did not want to get close enough to touch or scrub them. This started as we threw buckets of water on the floors and walls to clean up 2 or 3 times a day. Long handled brushes were used. Many times we thought if we made the clean up unpleasant, then they would quit doing it, but they did not. We had a choice of cold, warm or hot water to use. Basically, we never chose the middle. Many times we had a hard time getting hot, so cold was usually our choice. It inflicted the most pain and a scrubbing with a stiff brush would produce the desired effects we sought.

We were asked occasionally, but not often, about the bruises, sores or cuts on the patients; though it was never hard to convince others that the insane did it to themselves or other patients did it to them. Questions were rarely asked about the treatment of patients in the locked down dorms. Heavy doors were locked at night and a guard stayed between the two dorms. Doors were opened in the morning and you basically started over with counting; how many nuts you had, and how many deaths at night. It was always a good feeling for the staff when one died in the night, although he/she was almost always replaced. We somehow believed that we were advancing in our direction and that the replacement was not as bad as the original.

In all of my days there, I was not aware of male on male sex between staff and patient. I heard of some occurrences, but I was not made aware of them directly. I did catch some patients butt humping each other, but beatings and separation helped that. I often beat them myself, and I know this feeling was shared as there were normally 2-3 staff members per ward, per shift, who had chances to discuss things some. We believed that they were retarded and that death was best for them since we believed they somehow deserved to be mistreated.

When food was brought up to our ward, many patients were aware of the need to eat, but could not feed themselves. On rare occasions, nurses in training would come to help with feeding and the patients were treated well, but more often than not, we were there on our own. We felt that if they were too stupid to eat, then they should die. Food was often left on the carts and patients suffered as we made little attempt to feed them. Sickness and starvation was normal in our wards. No attempts to reach these people were made. No medications other than some laudanum or opium were used to calm the aggressive. This was nothing more than a place for them to be contained and a problem removed from the general public and kept out of sight.

My shift was different. Sometimes I worked 6-8 hour days, with Sunday off, sometimes 6-10 hour days. It was rarely night watch as I was trained to interact and restrain, and that was where I was kept. I could not help thinking how very little difference there was between them and me, other than the fact that I shit where I should and kept my clothes on, but I was one of them. I lived with them and I was locked up with them, but basically I was a nut that was getting paid to be a nut. I often felt that and I expressed this feeling, even though I was not crazy, I was staff. Left there long enough, I, too, would've thrown my shit on the walls.

Our staff was cycled as this pressure got to almost everyone, me included. This was the undesirable job that I had. Other staff referred to us as the "Nut Peddlers." This was a reference to those street peddlers selling roasted nuts, I guess. Nobody wanted our jobs, so relief was very seldom. We all would have gladly jumped at the chance if we were asked to move to another station. I believe that the asylum directors knew the difficulty to hire staff to help us and that our job was not the type one ever volunteered for. This is how I believe the following came about:

Often we were officially asked to help out in the women's wards, almost always at evening before bedtime lockdown. I was told, as others, that one or two were needed to help the women staff with threats of violence. Extra help was required because of the threats. I was allowed to stand and watch as women bathed and showered. I was not alone as female staff was present with belts, small cane switches and other items. The female staff was also under the same mental exhaustion as many of the male staff, as I recognized the symptoms. Beatings occurred for no real serious reasons; they seemed to be random and unprovoked. Many were not severe either. It seemed that light smacks or swats to line up patients somehow produced satisfaction in the staff.

The female dorms had the same levels of severity as we shared. I was called to the floors that were not as bad as mine. Many of these patients possessed some qualities of normal women. They would cover themselves (somewhat). They seemed to be concerned about their hair and looks. Some would talk or interact on various levels. This was very confusing because you could stand with two fully-grown women; one would talk and behave like a child and carry a doll, the other would drool or bark and growl like a dog. Application of the laws of society and what was right and normal never applied at Athens.

I believed that liberties were taken and decisions were abused because what started as only being on watch, turned into a disciplinary role. I believed that others and I were not easily replaced, so the staff directors did what they could to keep us there and in place. Often a female staff member would tell me that a patient was locked in a room and required discipline. I was sent into a room with a leather strap and saw women in a corner with no furniture whatsoever. I was told to change her spirit, break it if necessary, at my own discretion. Then the door would close and I went to work.

Power over another is an aphrodisiac for certain people. I would beat women for no reason that I would be aware of. No offense was made to me. I performed what I was told. What began as slight adjustments soon became all out barbaric beatings. Feelings were released within me that I knew never existed before coming to the asylum. I beat women with clothes on, then with clothes off. I tied them to the walls sometimes. I liked resistance, as it made me beat them harder. This spirit breaking soon developed into a beating followed by a sexual encounter. Once I entered a room that had two beds with mattresses with two women on their knees bent over the side of the bed with one hand tied to the foot of the bed, one hand tied to the head of the bed and their gowns pulled up over their heads. As I entered the room for the treatment, I was told a saying heard and said many times, "What happens in Athens stays in Athens." Then the door was closed behind me until I accomplished the "treatment."

What was peculiar was the fact that I never, ever talked with the patients, since I felt that they were all crazy and on a level with an animal, like a dog. This was not just my own assumption, but a feeling shared by many at the asylum. I worked on many women throughout my employment, but what I noticed was that none were ever singled out. The treatments I fulfilled were random throughout the women's wards. There was and always will be a very fine line as to who a patient is and who a staff member is. Generally, it is only the clothes one wears. One thought that would convey the feeding of patients: I remember thinking, "if they do not eat, they will not shit." It was all connected to the breakdown of our inner walls; the walls that separate good from bad, walls that keep us in line, walls that basically keep us from being them.

I am indeed in Ted's Group. I am here because the very ones I mistreated are here. I am not of an evil energy, so I am allowed to be here. Levels of love are so much higher here in the non-physical than with you. I started out with a task while on earth and somewhere along the line I allowed choices that did not support my original goal. Things were learned and I failed in areas that I most likely need to look at again. Situations arise and choices need to be made, right or wrong will be determined later, but my center was still pure. I am part of this group because of the change and outcome desired. I was never more a part of events than those receiving them. Things are to be learned, but never will they be learned from if they are forever hidden. This work is not to get anyone in trouble, not to shame any individual, but simply to establish a basis for truth. The asylum was nothing like it was portrayed, but a look into humanity as a whole might help those still seeking answers to one of life's most difficult questions: Why?

No decent treatment given to any patients there was ever made known to me. This was indeed a house of torture; a prison, but also a garbage can for Ohio. All unwanted souls were sent there and discarded to a dump (cemetery), but nonetheless, out of society's sight. I can tell you what I know. I know that Ohio University and the medical laboratory studies formed an alliance with Athens Asylum for the Insane for a couple of reasons; the most obvious was that as soon as a patient was pronounced dead, they would be whisked away to old Ohio University Labs, where being of "insane mind" would require the top of their heads to be sliced off to look at and study the brain of a "nut." Once these studies were done, the bodies would be sent back for burial. This was accomplished without consent from the families, as many families did not want them anyway.

Having been trained in movement and restraint, I was often called upon to help medical staff that was often present to restrain and prepare patients for treatment. Many forms of treatment were performed at the asylum, some very invasive and radical to say the least. Treatment at the asylum on subhuman subjects never followed any guidelines that often accompany normal patients. Many died. Many died painful, neglectful or unnecessary deaths. To be cured was great, but to die would be great for them too, as they would no longer be a burden. There never seemed to be a shortage of the supply of nut cases either, as 1200-1400 people always seemed to be in attendance.

The mildly insane received mildly intense treatments. The severely insane received radically severe treatments to cure or liberate them. The risk factor and rules normally followed by doctors did not apply. The criminally insane often received nothing less than torture with no real desire to cure or fix the insanity plagues they possessed. Many times, the severe criminally insane are dark energies. They are not and could never be here in Heaven with us. They were allowed, as is often the case, to intermingle on earth and could only be differentiated by their fruits, but those energies are forever forbidden from entering the same gates.

Treatments were as vague as the diagnosis or the understanding of the illnesses. It was a blatant guessing game. Nobody had a clue what caused the brain to operate in the manner we observed. Without understanding or knowing the cause, how could anyone begin to pretend to know the cure?

Earlier some believed that insanity was the devil manifesting himself in the body of an individual, so treatment was to open the body and let him out. It sounds ignorant, I know, but is it really? They would open the head, blood or cavity to allow Satan to leave the body. Well it worked, because as the Devil would leave, the subject would no longer possess the symptoms of insanity or life for that matter. Have we changed from then to now? Not much in my opinion. We are still just as in the dark about this illness now as we were then.

It became popular belief that people with symptoms of insanity were simply allowed to slowly develop and stray from normal ways of behavior, so a very simple treatment practice would jolt them back to reality. Jolting became the focus for many methods of treatment; this involved electro-shock. Earlier than that, jolts to the head were meant to shake the brain and all of a sudden the patient would wake up from their stupidity. The problem here was that not one case I was ever involved in EVER resulted in anyone becoming "normal." At best, I would find people killed or placed into a state of lethargy that ultimately would result in death, due to the patient's inability to perform even the simplest of daily functions. We would just move on to the next case since this group of people was nothing more than a burden in the asylum and most directly, in many cases, part of the work force.

I remember two treatments probably not found in too many books, but sure to be found in doctors' notes somewhere. Occasionally, I would perform shock therapy on patients as follows: the patient would often sit in a chair, blindfolded as to deter any flinching. I would stand directly behind and aside with the doctor and nursing staff present. I was instructed to take a small board about 4 inches wide and 30 inches long, with a rounded handle. This board would be normally ¾ of an inch in thickness. With most all of my might, I would slap the patient in the back of the head with the flat of the board. The idea was to jolt the brain in such a way as to stimulate normal behavior almost immediately.

I performed this procedure about twenty times on all males, and two times on females and we never achieved the results they were seeking. In about four of these instances the patient died immediately. One time I split the man's head open. In one instance the patient was not blindfolded and an eyeball was forced from the socket. Many times the patient, although not dead initially, was placed in such a state of helplessness that eating, sleeping and drinking did not occur and death lingered, but eventually came. In one case the patient was placed hanging by his feet above the floor with his arms tied, then he was allowed to fall to the floor rapidly to achieve the wellness. I was never trained as a doctor, but even I knew that he wouldn't survive. I think he broke his neck. A few treatments with a spring-loaded ramming device were used on the forehead as a means of separating the front part of the brain. Again, this was ineffective. These treatments were often saved for the severely or mildly insane.

The criminally insane were usually saved for severe treatments that were known to produce painful results, but not usually intended to cure anything. Jolting was the goal. Doctors believed that you could suddenly regain your senses through a quick blow to your consciousness. Bath therapy was another form of treatment. I was asked to bind and restrain a naked patient and place them in a bathtub. The tub was filled with cold water and then ice. Often towels with ice were placed on the head as well. I tied their arms behind their back and to a ring on the floor of the tub. A board was often placed over the tub. I witnessed convulsions so severe that they knocked the boards off the top. I saw people turn blue (their lips and skin). I saw people pass out and some never regained their wits again. The idea was to take the patient to almost death and then let them back. The problem was that no doctors knew when death was close or not.

"...the patient would often sit in a chair, blindfolded as to deter any flinching"

We also saw treatments using the same idea, only using hot water. The patients were virtually boiled alive as water was heated to almost boiling. These patients were almost always gagged. That never worked either. Since the cold bath never worked, the idea came about that they would leave the patient in the ice water only 15 minutes instead of one hour, but we would add a small mild electro shock to their heads to help speed up the process. Nope, it didn't work either in any case I observed or heard about. We sometimes tied a patient to a bed wrapped in sheets, poured cold water over them and then packed them in ice; this was another version and no positive results were ever mentioned.

Pain was inflicted in all sorts of treatments. The ideas were that the patient would experience such great pain that he would just snap back to reality. None of these treatments ever cured anyone of epilepsy, depression, schizophrenia, etc.

Remember not all that is known will be translated because of the depth of humankind's depravity. It is never pleasant for neither the giving nor the receiving. The events spoken and relayed are actual events. My part is to tell about the involvement that I participated in. These events were forever hidden and forgotten behind the beautiful brick towers covered up by the magnificent landscaping and justified by nothing. There are few that know of the holes in the stories. These few will find comfort in the answers to the nagging questions that have lingered for years about loved ones and forgotten family members. Branches on family trees can now be assigned a name. Mourning can take place, and knowing that the animals that we took care of and viewed were in fact integral parts to family units and history. Even if the impact on the earth by these souls may not have been great, it was real, definite and important to humanity. Large or small, they all counted. I offer the stories to be translated from the section of time that I was at the asylum. I was aware of events through my involvement and knowledge, although perhaps not directly involved in certain events.

I will interject my thoughts at times as I have formed opinions about some events. I was not an educated man. I had almost 7 years of formal education. My family realized that it was hard to have food on the table while able boys were looking at books and stacking numbers. Although we all knew that educated people would gain later, we understood that if we pursued education now it meant we would eat later as well, so I started working at 11-12 years of age. My insights to you are not thoughts of an educated opinion, only a simple expression of my understanding, so please receive it in this manner.

"These events were forever hidden and forgotten behind the beautiful brick towers covered up by the magnificent landscaping and justified by nothing."

Getting back to the jolt experience, I never saw it work in any cases that I was aware of. Doctors would talk amongst themselves of cases that showed improvement in other cities. Doctors were receiving desirable and lasting results with patients in Chicago and New York (not any in Athens). After all the jolting to the brain simultaneously, experiences in severe pain were administered. As mentioned earlier, details of these examples as decided by the group would be concealed, due to the senseless nature of them all. This was the consensus of those receiving the treatment and the vote was unanimous, so we will only express to you that this extension of the jolt theory created infections, amputations, and most often death. Severe middle stage insane cases and most criminally insane were the subjects.

In my opinion I remained a small educated man by books, but in no way was I ever thought of as stupid. I could not help thinking that should these doctors remove the coat and pin they strutted around in, you would find it hard to differentiate them from the lower level east wing criminals we called insane. Similar events seem to be shared by both groups. Some were caught and some were paid for their behavior. You make sense of it, because I have not been able to.

The insane asylum was extremely intricate in design and complicated in overall operation. We would receive patients daily, sometimes up to 5 per day and they would admit at different levels of need. Severe would become more severely damaged, and the mild would end up severely damaged. Often a patient would arrive for a short stay with the original intent to take some time to receive some treatment and to get better. All too often, this idea would be abandoned early. Family members were grateful that they got them there in time, as they were so close on the verge of cracking. How stupid was that? Nobody ever realized or thought that perhaps the asylum (we) helped them over the line from mild insanity to severe lunacy.

I often believed that should we walk down the street of downtown Athens and pick up any prominent well-thinking citizen, remove their clothes and all forms of dignity, treat them as an animal and a bi-product of humanity, rape them regularly and abuse them frequently, given 1-2 weeks tops I could create a patient at the Athens Lunatic Asylum of ANY of those well-minded people (my thoughts only though).

How was funding obtained? How was it covered up? Why were there never investigations of treatment? Not one nut could ever testify. Who would believe the word of someone that didn't bathe, smelled like piss, did not comb their hair and systematically could not focus enough to carry on a conversation? Would their word ever be considered over that of the educated staff, administrators or the highly regarded doctors? Nurses did not tell because it was hard enough for women to find work in the little doctor circles and they would be blackballed and never find work anywhere. Doctors carried the support of the community to fix the crazy people and did whatever it took to achieve this. Any patient that decided to speak out in any way would be moved up the list of the severely insane. And guess what? They would stop talking almost immediately.

A look at "Cottage M": This is significant as to the funding and cover up of the asylum. This became known as the "Crazy Cat House." Female patients were rotated through this house to fulfill and perform all needs of perversion. It seemed that nobody was immune to the rotation. Young, old, very old, crippled; if they had a hole, it was used. In return, large amounts of funding were filed through the asylum on a regular basis!!

I never recalled seeing any women coming to Athens to cum. It was all men: men in suits and derbies, flashy and prominent men. What is it with men? I know not all of these men were without wives. What was the draw to overpower a woman that was tied up or unable to say no? They were not exposed to the anger, circumstances and rage that we were daily. They paid for their experience. I am in no way justifying my behavior, but I am able to follow the progressive step that led me to that point.

A room in the west wing of the main female ward was set up to perform abortions. Often girls as young as 12 years old were sent here to be liberated of their own shame or the shame they brought to their families. Do you realize how twisted this was? These young girls were accused of bringing shame to their families! Often these girls were raped by a family member resulting in pregnancy and yet *they* were the ones that brought shame to the family. I swear this whole circle is fucked up!!

We received scared young girls to fix and we did fix them. They were worked into the rotation of the "Crazy Cat House" even with the baby. I found it odd that even the fat, ugly girls were sought after and requested. Once the girls really started to show the growth of the child, an abortion was performed and they were "liberated." What should have taken only a few weeks to a month at most to rectify under normal circumstances, was easily written off to the trauma of the event keeping them sometimes for 1 to 2 years, (depending on the insistence of the family to recover them) so that when they would return home, mostly in a catatonic state and even try to relay the events, families would view it as just punishment for being a slut or harlot and refused to entertain any truth of relayed events. The performing of the abortions generally left the women/girls unable to ever have children. The events surrounding the liberation left them unwilling to ever perform normally as a woman.

The farm laborers were instructed to continually keep brush/scrap lumber piled. This was where many unborn infants were taken to be burned. Later in 1905, there was a coal-fired furnace that produced heat and water. That was where we took young ones to be incinerated.

I personally, observed the mistreatment of patients who were chained (shackled) in the lower levels. You have been made aware of the extreme neglect and abuse that I observed and many times participated in. I know for a fact that most violent or criminally insane patients had to have something done to them. Normally the criminals already caught would be hanged or shot, but if they proved they were crazy, then they were not responsible for the things they did to others, but something needed to be done, so they were sent to us.

Since we were unable to let them roam with the regulars or the staff, they were isolated. None ever seemed to have guests to call on them, so they were often kept in the lower level of the men's wing. Since I was trained to restrain and subdue unruly patients, I was involved in the placement or removal of patients so I know for a fact they were chained either by one leg or one hand to the wall.

Treatment of these men was animal-like, and they were always treated and referred to as a level lower than human.

I remember one incident where one of these men had badly rotted teeth and the pus and stench was so bad that something had to be done. This inmate kept trying to bite anyone coming close to him, so I was asked to help restrain him. I also remember the visiting doctor pulling out 4 of his rotting teeth and never giving him whiskey or nothing. I wondered what it would be like if we had changed spots and how I would've reacted, but the thought quickly faded when I thought of the ones he killed in order to be placed here. That, coupled with the fact that he looked inhuman, smelled worse and behaved like an animal, made it so my thoughts of compassion quickly left me. The lower levels were very dark. The only light was from lower windows and not all areas were lit. I never remembered any women treated in this way; perhaps they did not commit crimes so hideous as to allow them to be in this predicament. I recall going down to help hold a patient with infected wounds to be doctored again. As I got closer and began to restrain this man, I noticed in fact that the sores on his heels and lower legs were covered in maggots. The doctor used alcohol to remove them and the man screamed quite a lot. Two things I found interesting; that man lived quite a while and the maggots returned after two days.

Things were difficult here and never easy. I experienced many things and many I would not like to remember. The maggots did not seem to ever bother me much as they were not partial to just the lower levels; it was a constant occurrence to find patients with maggots crawling on open sores. I did not like my stay at the asylum. I was paid well and stayed as I possessed no other marketable skills and work was not in abundance.

Red

"...I personally, observed the mistreatment of patients who were chained (shackled) in the lower levels."

Chapter Three

Hello, I was at Athens Asylum for the Insane. I was placed there at the early age of 7 years old. I lived with my Aunt Lydia and Uncle Joseph, although he was only my uncle because he married Aunt Lydia. I was born with the inability to speak. I could not communicate verbally at all, and nobody could communicate with me. I was sent to what was referred to as the Athens Hospital as they did know what to do with me. I was born just outside of Portsmouth, Ohio. My father was never around and my mother drank and conducted herself in a manner unfit for a lady, so my aunt Lydia raised me for 5 years. Although they were good people, they were always poor. Uncle Joe worked in the coal yards in Kentucky and was home every other weekend. Times were hard and I am sure that my aunt and uncle thought they were doing what would ultimately be the best for me.

I worked as soon as I arrived in Athens. I never knew it was an asylum for the insane until I was about 9 years old. I worked in two jobs mostly and sometimes in the bakery. I loved to work there since I loved the smell of bread. All I did there was help wash bread pans or cut bread into four pieces. It was not very hard work, but it was always hot. I worked mostly in the laundry room folding sheets and gowns (lots of each). We always had large loads of laundry. The ladies I worked with were kind to me. I worked in the garden picking vegetables and would go there with Anita and Beth-Ann mostly. They were nice to me also.

There were other kids there off and on. If they got to be 12 years old, they would leave and not come to work again. I had a friend named Della. She was born with no arms at all. She smiled big and had gold hair. I helped her eat and pee and comb her hair. She only smiled a lot, but really could not do much more. Nurses came to visit often. One was really nice to me and talked a lot to me. She found out that I could hear and do what was asked of me and that I was not stupid; I just could not make words with my mouth. She taught me to talk by making words with my hands. We had conversations and she could understand me. It was the first time ever that someone could listen to me.

I never attended school, so from the age of 8 to 9 I learned to make letters. Spelling words was very hard. I had words that were pictures and I would group them together because spelling was very slow for me. The nurse I liked a lot who helped me and listened to my hands was Mae Zwingly. When I was 10 ½ years old I got sick. I got bad diarrhea and high fevers. The fevers were low and high and eventually, after almost 3 weeks, I passed over. I am not buried in any of the formal cemeteries, but I am located on the grounds.

Sarah Jensen

Chapter Four

I AM RILEY. I WAS A HIRED hand at the asylum. I was born and raised up in Ironton and found work at Athens. The day I stepped foot on that farm, I was reminded that it was a self-supportive city and that everything we needed was here. That was the idea, but nobody had to say a word. You just knew that things lacked and were not quite what the superintendent said they were. I was told that this was the best job on earth. It was not. It was not much more than what I left at home, the only difference was I got paid. I did all farm jobs. Others were hired for trade jobs, as the skill matched the pay. I knew farming and that was how I was hired on. This place had a pile of cows that were milked twice daily. I was not head of the milking crew, but helped out often. I plowed, fed, cut, harvested, planted, weeded, and cultivated.

I worked on a huge 1,000-acre farm; all state-backed with healthy stock and updated equipment. I liked my work and the people I worked with. We bought a lot from town folks though. I liked working at the asylum farm, as it was honest, clean work. Clean meaning that we kept our machinery up to date and all of the grounds were very well kept. The barns were cleaned on a regular basis. I was young and in my 20s with everything that anyone wanted right here. We lived in the bunk house for farm laborers.

At first, the supers tried to have us work the nuts. I have to admit, some worked out, but very few did. We would give them jobs that did not amount to much since they were really not very helpful when you thought about it. They picked apples (off the ground). Sometimes they hauled branches off to burn after pruning trees in the orchard. We once had males and females pick up potatoes after digging. That was a nightmare; they threw the potatoes, took a bite out of them, put 6 or 8 in a bag, or just sat and dug holes in the dirt. It was hard to work or communicate with them. The ones that would or could carry on a conversation said things like, "I am a millionaire," or told completely fanciful and colorful stories.

I cannot say much about the goings-on at the asylum. I worked all the time so I did not see very many patients. I saw some patients, but only very few. Mostly I saw patients walking or sitting on the grounds with visitors. As far as day-to-day contact, there were very few occasions.

Riley

Margaret Schilling's Stain

Chapter Five

I am Mary, you know me mostly by Margaret Schilling. Nobody ever called me Margaret. I find it funny as to what it takes to become a legend. Not much, I guess. No more than a rot spot or stain.

I attended Athens for a number of reasons. I found myself to be compulsive and depressed at times. I also was somewhat of a skits-o-frantic as I believed people were always talking about me. Those of you that are aware of my story should know that many of the facts are not correct. You will make sense of some points on your own and some I will point out. Yes, I had a terrible addiction to cigarettes, and they were very hard to get as a patient. So believe me when I would get one, it was as if someone handed me a stick of gold. I became friends with a few of the attendants and being a mature woman I was aware of what a woman could do to receive almost anything in the world. So, in exchange for sexual favors, I would receive a number of items. Cigarettes being the most important, but I would also receive and ask for whiskey and even perfume on occasions. This exchange went on for some time and was quite agreeable to all parties involved. The exchange of sex happened often and in many locations throughout the hospital..

Doug: Mary, this is very difficult for me to write. May I print?

(Berta's comment: Mary made Doug write in cursive as he received her story...He does not know how to write in cursive! He was struggling with it.)

Mary: I know you like to print, but you need the practice and look at how well you are doing!!

Doug: Not Funny!

Mary: Okay, Cry Baby. If you need to, go ahead and print! Just tell it right, okay?

Doug: Okay.

Sex was a regular thing and occurred often and in many locations. It started with the night shift attendant and as others heard that a piece of pussy could be had for a pack of cigarettes, they joined the boat. The sex industry of "Cottage M" had come to an end by the time I was at the asylum, but sex and abuse were ever still present, just perhaps not as an organized sport as it had been, so I did well. All but one was decent to me. Most just jumped on, got their kicks, rolled off and I got my smokes, but one day a guy was rough. He treated me like a dog. He always took me from behind and wanted only my behind, that is how he liked it, and that is how things went bad. This one man did not like the fact that he was sharing me with three other men at that time. Especially when he started it, he felt as if I somehow belonged to him.

The events that led me to being a legend, if you will, was the night that this attendant took me to the tower for his daily fill of animal sex. He told me to completely undress, which he often did. Due to my compulsive tendencies, I neatly folded my clothes and shoes in an orderly stack. Then, he too undressed and began treating me as a dog (again). He became more and more violent, smacking, spanking and choking me. He never did ejaculate; he just kept entering me time and time again but he seemed to spend more and more time around my neck area, and then he would not let go. I tried to fight, but he was on me, in me, and held my arms above my head with one hand and choked me with the other. I remember dying. I remember the release I felt. I remember stopping my struggle. The feeling of freedom was so multi-level that its rush to my senses was unbelievable, like a feeling of "finally."

"...I remember dying. I remember the release I felt. I remember stopping my struggle."

I did not need to smoke anymore. I did not need to worry about people talking about me. I did not need to worry about who was going to hump me tonight. I did not need medication. I did not need to feel as if something was wrong with me. I was free and that was an incredible feeling.

This man felt bad for killing me, but what did he think he was doing? It's like going fishing and feeling bad when you catch a fish! When you choke someone, they are bound to die, don't you think? Regardless, I know he felt bad, but I felt great. I didn't much like the way my body and hair looked anyway, so he, in a manner of speaking, delivered me. He laid me out on the floor; he folded my hands across my stomach and left my clothes by my side. He even straightened my hair before he left me. I can't explain what happened, other than I was left on a concrete floor in the December/January months to rot. The natural process of body decay is probably what stained the open pores of the cement, but you really don't need to have an imagination to see the outline of my body.

Now the story goes that even after many attempts to scrub the floor where I was laying (excuse me, but that was one attempt) the stain could not be removed. If I had in fact wandered off to an abandoned part of the hospital, why would they bother cleaning the floor so much? As Doug figured out, if I would have died on my own, I would not have been lying flat out; I would have been curled up in a ball. Furthermore, even flat out crazy people don't take their clothes off and freeze to death. Sorry! Yeah, it was a cover up and an embarrassment that was hard to hide, but once again, it was a crazy loon against the trained and qualified staff of the Athens Mental Institution and well… you know whose story was going to prevail.

Mary Schilling

Chapter Six

Hello, I am Raymond. I was hired as an attendant at Athens Lunatic Asylum. I did not last long as an attendant and heard word that an opening was available for grounds work and light farming, so I transferred. I was a large black man and had no family, so I stayed on the grounds.

I was the man that a scrawny little chicken necked white boy named Slim talked about. He was special to me and assigned to me. He did everything he could do to stay away from the main buildings. He only went there to sleep as he had a bed check, but that runt wouldn't even eat there in the dining halls. That place scared the tar out of him. I knew that he occasionally had these fits. Not knowing what they were called, but it didn't take a whole lot of smarts to know how to help him and to know that this feller was not crazy. Yes, he had something wild going on with his nut, but most of the time was just a great kid. He was willing to learn and loved to read even though he could not write so good.

I was glad to help him and worked with him for a while. It would break my heart to see him wander off to the ward to sleep, but come first light, he was up and knocking on my door. You know as far as treatment for him, the stick in his mouth was his idea as he told me later after a fit that he felt as if his teeth would crack and his jaws explode for as tight as he would clench his teeth. Well, we both got that idea and I carried a small dowel in my pocket whenever he was with me. The rest was nothing more than treating someone as the right way of doing things. You see, I cared about this boy, and that's what I did. Whenever I saw a fit of his coming out of him, I would grab my stick, put it in his teeth and let him on the ground because that's where he was going anyway. Then I would usually sit astride him with my legs so I could keep him from going side to side. I would hold his hands gently, so he wouldn't hit himself. That boy would go wild sometimes and for my 275-pound frame sometimes it was hard to hang on, but I did. Soon he'd come around again. I'd get him up and then help him get cleaned up, as most times (I am sure he don't mind I tell you) he'd mess his drawers. I'd go help him get back together and we'd go back out to work.

We could sometimes go for maybe two months until it would happen again. Lots of people were scared by his actions and I must admit that it was something else the first time I saw them too, but that boy can't be crazy for only about 10 minutes out of a day and be right the rest of the time. So I guess I was like a doctor there with my very own patient named Slim. The scrawniest excuse for a little white boy I ever saw.

We did most everything at the asylum. We picked up sticks, trimmed trees, raked drives, tended flowerbeds and sometimes we would help with the piglets, as he loved being with them things. I teased him all the time 'cause I think he liked them and the runt 'cause that's what he was too, a runt.

Raymond

Women's Wing

Chapter Seven

I AM ETTA GABRIEL. MY PART AT The Athens Lunatic Asylum was somewhat earlier. I worked day shift and some nights. I never really liked nights. The pay was not as good, but more than that, I was bored as we would use laudanum to sedate the patients at night and lock them down knowing that they were unable to slip through the grille work. They would be there in the morning, so at night there was very little to be done in the way of tasks. We would only walk the halls twice at night in a shift to check and see if any were hanging from the ceilings, which was quite a silly thing to do as there was nothing to suspend from. So in most ways it was a very boring job. Night shift amounted to reading, playing cards, drinking whiskey or the occasional mixing with male attendants, but never me.

I came to The Athens Asylum wanting to help. I wanted to further my training and go into full nursing, but nursing school was hard to get into in the 1870s and this was the closest I could get without formal training. Attending school meant spending large tuition money (which I did not have). So hiring on as a nursing attendant, I was actually getting paid to nurse without going to school, and that was my idea.

I saw many things at the asylum and heard even more. A lot was quite disturbing and very little was of any comfort that left you with an abundant feeling of hope, but I did what I could.

I was chosen and attracted at the same time to participate in this work with both Doug and Berta, as well as with Ted's group. I am sure you are aware that there were varying levels of patients at the asylum. I was, mostly by choice, assigned to the stage two patients. Stage three and up meant you had to be a bit crazy yourself in order to work on the locked down wards or floors.

I honestly wanted to make a difference (in the beginning). I wanted to see a patient respond to the tender care I would provide, stand up, get dressed and walk out the front gate and wave to me and say thank you. That is the truth. That is what was in my head as I was signing the papers for employment. I never really knew how deeply disturbed some of these people were or realize how different each would act and how that would determine the direction of treatment that we had to carry out. Some would need firm direction and restraints at times. Some you would need to keep sedated with laudanum. Some only needed to be touched and talked to kindly and softly. Other times, if you merely touched a woman on the shoulder, she would scream and run to escape you, but you were supposed to know these patients and were expected to switch your approach in an instant. Sometimes you had to administer two types of procedures simultaneously. It was hard and the training we received was not ever written, only known by doing.

I, as well as others in Ted's Group, will offer objection and will comment to the article that Doug read in research. The article stated that the asylum's utmost goal was the utter and total care of the patients. Well, I need to say that I knew that if a patient was at the asylum, we received money from the state for each head that was there, other than those being totally supported by funds from family. So if one left, so did the funds. It was not our goal to keep them sick, but we did not greatly encourage any reason to get better and leave. We often felt like a holding facility.

The other point was the mention of walk-aways. I am not aware of much of this. The stage three and above patients were hard to handle, so they often wore no shoes and sometimes gowns. Stage or level two, which was my care, wore clothes, but had no personal effects; no money, jewelry, papers etc. How could someone wander off, go to town and try to accomplish anything? They could not get a train ticket without money, possibly hitch a ride I guess, but then, where would they go? Home to the very ones that put them there? All of Athens was on high advisory and watch constantly. The asylum had its own police force, if you will. They would come to the attention of anyone "acting a little off." The sheriff would hold them and the Athens Asylum guys would pick them up, so walk-aways were not something I ever saw.

There was never any occasion for anyone to go to town as the asylum had it all. If it was not here, it would be brought in, so hitching a ride on a wagon to town only to slip away was not a good plan either. There were the level one people and yes, they were very well behaved, only mildly slow or suffered from drinking too much and at admittance would be a level two or three only until they could control the urge to drink in excess. Eventually they would get to a level one and believe it or not, I did see some patients (quite a few really) leave and go back home, but remember that once there it was hard for the asylum to let them go due to funding. It seemed that the asylum wanted to make absolutely sure they were well before they let them go.

Level one group could go to town on occasion with guides and it was all planned. The family members would be alerted and small monies were sent and people could go get combs, shoelaces, new undergarments, ribbons, etc. but mostly it was a gesture, not actually a benefit.

What I offer to this work is only daily accounts of the lives of patients and the attendants. As stated before, we still have the shell visible. We have some facts confused in some cases. We have legends (blown up mostly that's why they are legends) but what does seem to be missing is the life or heart of this section of history. It can't be changed as nobody can go back and make changes, but rather to help it be known that the people on both sides of the asylum were just that, people. They were important, each in their own way. I saw life a certain way and through a certain set of views, but patients saw the same experiences, only in a different way. Different things were important to me than was to them. I never remember watching dust dance on a windowsill when the sun shown through the grilles, but I knew some that waited each day for this event. Does that mean they were crazy? Perhaps by my missing this event made me the crazy one. Perhaps I should have given the keys to the patients and had them lock me up? I wonder about this. I knew some patients that could tell you how many square tiles were placed on the floor of some halls, why, because they bothered to take the time to count them. I merely walked over them and hardly was aware of the surface of the floors. I often wondered, as I kept my thoughts mainly to myself about the patients, what led them to be placed here and is it really that bad that they pay so much attention to the little things in life that we pay so little attention to?

I am so sad at times when I realize so many on my floor, I mean if you really think about it, didn't need Athens Insane Asylum to help them. Sometimes I believe they didn't really need help at all, but just perhaps a little understanding. I once asked a woman what she waited for and why she had such a pleasant flush across her face as she looked from the window each morning. When she told me of the dancing dust she watched for, I looked in the same direction and I noticed the same show she was so intrigued by. My only thoughts were that I was glad that I, too, became mystically drawn and captivated by its beauty. The scary thing to me was thinking, what was the difference between these two women looking toward the window for the same morning show of beauty?

"...I knew some patients that could tell you how many square tiles were placed on the floor of some halls"

"...When she told me of the dancing dust she watched for, I looked in the same direction and I noticed the same show she was so intrigued by"

I really didn't intend to ramble on, but I really wanted to give an account of the food here at Athens Asylum. Sometimes there would be as many as 1,200 to 1,300 patients housed here. Then there was the support staff, attendants, farm hands, and grounds workers. An incredible amount of people that had to be fed three times a day, every single day with no days off. People have to eat every day. So do you ever really think about this? Though the staff received different food from the patients and the farm hands and outside help was also different from us, there was an enormous amount of cooking being done each day. Male wards had their own cooks, female wards had their own cooks and outside help had their own cooks. Feeding 1200 people a meal one day of potatoes would come to around 1000 potatoes per sitting. So imagine if chicken, turkey, pork or beef was to be served?

A lot of bread was baked in very large amounts. Most often a gruel or stew or combination of the two was prepared. Vegetables and small amounts of meat on occasion would be cooked in very large pots. Bread was served with almost each meal as economic filler. Everything was dictated by levels. The better food and combinations would be served to the staff and as you went to the higher levels the quality of food seemed to diminish. For instance, levels one and two would get a stew with vegetables and some hint of meat. Levels three and four would get the same with little meat and flour added to thicken, and often would receive bread from a day or two before. Level five, which were the violent and criminals, would receive only bare minimums of nutrition, as many believed they were doing them no help by allowing them to continue to live so their food was cold and often stale or left over (of very poor quality and little nutritional value, in my opinion). Fresh milk was very limited as the dairy was very young and growing. This was mostly reserved for the staff and the lower levels. Beef was raised and mostly ground to aid in stretching it. Poultry was brought in from outside and almost always a treat for the staff. I believe that the asylum did the very best they could in order to feed that many people day in and day out. You can only imagine how these kitchens worked tirelessly from one meal to the next. It was a very impressive operation to view, and they are to be commended for their efforts.

We shall now touch on the subject of clothing. The time segment I speak of is from 1874-1890s and with this in mind, I hope you will entertain these happenings. Often a patient came to us with one or two small bags, but this is relative to the individual. In those bags would be two changes of clothes, socks, underclothes, a coat and perhaps a toothbrush, hairbrush, shaving equipment, ribbons, a hat, books, paper and pencil, and even a picture or two. This was often the lower level patients, and this was more often silly, as if you were entering an insane asylum I am not sure they would let you bring in and keep a STRAIGHT RAZOR! Hat pins, jewelry or cash also were not allowed.

Athens Asylum was all new. All new ideas as to the daily care of our mentally ill neighbors and I believe that nobody (although they had ideas) really understood all of the little aspects of putting this together. Early good intentions seemed, as time passed, somewhat impractical and needed to step aside for practicality which always seemed to stand up straighter and out front. This was the case with just the small item of clothing. Originally, people could bring clothes and personal effects, to a point, of course. Originally, each patient was to have their own room with pictures on the walls and vases with fresh cut flowers, but as our numbers increased and the levels system was established, practicality took the forefront. Patients started to bring and wear their own clothes and problems arose. Let's say my ward for example, there could be as many as 45-60 women all on basically the same levels of ability, but levels of need were very different. Our facility was to house only 20-30 tops, so now we started to put 2-3 per room. If each patient in my care took their underclothes and put them to wash every two to three days and then top clothes two times a week: let's do the math, shall we? There was also the fine set of clothes that were kept back for visits. This was a very large pile of dirty laundry, now add that to the other floors and add the men's wards also. Is it possible to imagine what this would amount to? Now some more to think about; what do you think about mending? Who was to do that? We wouldn't be able to just keep a mending kit on our floor for everyone on different levels of needs to grab. What about clothes going to the laundry then coming back to its rightful owner? Were they to all need name tags? Some were here for months, while some for years.

You can see that very soon after our first patients arrived problems were right behind them as well. Struggles for the first year or two were difficult, so lots of meetings and very smart people with many ideas were helpful. It was very interesting to notice the procession of practicality as they started to try new things. It was intended that ladies of level two and higher would be able to have one set of clothes and we kept them in a room on a shelf with a number assigned to each. Then on occasions of going out or getting a visitor, the special day clothes could then be worn. This was fine and did seem to work well. Daily clothes were mostly gowns and at first a number was sewn inside to identify the owner, but as different sizes were available this did not last more than two months because with so many ladies and the mix up of numbers and such, we would spend half a day just trying to sort things out.

So here comes the practicality: the ladies were issued a gown. All sizes were one size, so if you were big, it might not cover all of you, but if you were small you might end up with two layers! There were no numbers. We would receive a shipment of clothes from the laundry daily, and send a load of foul laundry all tied up daily and this seemed to work well. On levels one and two there were some buttons but as with most they also disappeared. Do you realize we never mentioned bedding in those loads?

Athens Lunatic Asylum had its problems to overcome for which they did seem to do well. The intentions were well meant. The asylum was an absolutely amazing place and not very many people bothered to stop and take in what it really actually took to make it all work for just one day.

Shall I find contentment or solace in the expressions that I have relayed to those willing to hear? Or shall it be freedom with the release of the thoughts that have retained me for so long? I feel not the anxiety that such retention has confined me to a place in time or history as the words that I have spoken are the words that have been hidden in each heart that is willing to receive them. My words are those that have been questions and feelings that have been present only not recognized by emotion, for nothing has bound me to my allotment, nothing more than my desire to bring forth awareness of the relationships of the mind and the body. How complicated we tend to keep our relationships and how little we actually know of each other. How little is actually known by our own admissions and how easily we subdue the undesired from our experiences. Who actually sets the rules for the standards of mental illness? Who justifies the enforcements of such? Have these standards ever been observed? As the locations of the lines for which are crossed are generally and continually in motion. I never saw these lines, but did observe those that seemingly crossed then for the brief moment in history that I participated in.

Do I have the freedom to move along? Yes, in a sense; nothing is holding me here, nothing more than the sincere desire to convey my thoughts on such an undesirable topic; my thoughts of wonder, sadness, unknowing and of hope. Perhaps through these insights one might observe the differences of individuals through a different set of eyes and know that what lies before each of us through the course of life is difficult and challenging and through our direct choices of how to respond to these challenges will set the precedent for where the lines are to be found. Knowing that all souls I encountered began as good, only to respond to the events of life in a way deemed unsuitable for further existence at large. Please continue to exercise compassion on those that struggle as I did my best to do so as well.

Move along? Sure, as I have had the opportunity to complete what was unfinished in thought and you have the ability to complete what was unfinished by hand. We were all at the asylum at one time or another if not physically, then emotionally and it was all in part to where these lines were laid. I express these words to you in complete love, then, now and in the future. Please continue to strive for understanding.

Etta Gabriel

Chapter Eight

Hello, I am Emily Jarvis. I was a nursing intern at the asylum for only one month in the early part of 1891. I need to tell you that the place was all the rumors told of. I hated it and requested to be moved as soon as I could. There was very little that could be accomplished there. My placement was to help teach the learning nursing staff the fundamentals of human behavior, but most important was that we would learn to behave and care for those hurting and for those who really did not desire to have our help. We bathed and dressed them, combed their hair, dressed their wounds, and met all of the basic needs of a childlike person. I saw neither advancement, nor improvement in the four weeks I was there. My stay was supposed to be longer, but I insisted on being placed in another area. My desire was to work with children and infants, and even perhaps as a midwife in some way, so I benefited very little from my experience. I also wanted to mention that I was not aware of any children at the asylum for the duration of my service.

Emily Jarvis

Josiah Whipkey
1841-1881

Chapter Nine

Spotsylvania
Charlotte or Charlottesville
Dry Creek / Davis Creek
Vicksburg
Gettysburg
Wounded in calf and knee
Body parts in trees
Sad stacks of shoes
Never enough coffins
The ground is stained
Cold
Rain
No food
Stealing
Cannon balls bouncing
My feet and hands are cold
Temporary injury in my right eye
Trees splitting around me
Bullets sound like bees
So many prisoners are sad and scared
But mostly tired
Dead horses
Men apart, not together
Looks like butchering

Unbelievable
Jamie Hatley, good friend
Lost his head due to bouncing cannon ball
It took all of his head off of his shoulders
About 4-5 feet from me
He never even screamed
It just happened
Can't sleep no more
My ears ring always now
Scared of thunder and lightning
I am still always cold
I killed men and they didn't know it was me
I shot rebs and after would walk over and see they were only little boys
Nothing is right no more
A bullet will hit me and I don't know when
I don't long to love no more
I don't hate either
I just don't nothin' no more
I can't pray cause I am ashamed and don't know if it would matter
I am scared all the time
My insides won't be still
I don't cry like I used to
Men shouldn't cry like a baby
But you shouldn't drag your guts behind you
As you crawl through the mud either
Just lay down and die
I wish I could
I can't run
I wish I could fly
I don't hear so much now
They stand me up and tell me to kill some more
I have to
I hurt a lot

I want to write home
But can't
I am ashamed and don't feel it right to share what I see
Need to sleep
If I hide, they will find me
I just want to die, but don't want the hurting part
What are my choices?
War is worse than hell
Way worse
I used to love the snow
But it makes a dead man turn black overnight and his eyes like a dead deer
We saw a dog eating a dead Rebel's legs once and watched
We shot the dog 'cause it wasn't right
I saw a flower growing next to a dead man and I stared at them both
And was confused by the contrast
I went to Athens because my family thought it best
The smell of dead men never left my nose
The sights never left my eyes
I wanted to scream
I wanted to cry
I wanted to run
I wanted to tell
My body wouldn't let me
I wanted to rest
I wanted to forget
I thought I wanted to feel
But never did again
I looked up at nothing
I listened to nothing
I stopped praying
I wanted to die but feared the hurting part of it
I was treated good
But mostly left alone

Always
My sister would hold my hand
I couldn't hold hers back
I wanted to
But couldn't
Wasn't there supposed to be more?
I think I missed it
I am glad there wasn't more
I've had enough for me
I still can't fly
I don't hold on to nothin'
Yeah, I am ready
I think I had enough
I'll just stand here and listen to more of nothing

Josiah Whipkey
1841-1881

Chapter Ten

I WAS THE ONE THAT WROTE "I never was crazy" on the window ledge. Fact is I never was crazy. I was at Athens for six months for excessive alcohol dependency. In English: I was a drunk and I became agitated if I could not get to the level of numbness or drunkenness that I felt I needed to escape all of the circumstances surrounding my drunkenness, specifically my abused childhood mostly. The way a person is treated in their earlier years is so important to how they are to behave and react as an adult. This case goes for me because I was a mess as an adult. I lacked in so many areas of adult development. It was hard for me to adjust to being an adult so I didn't and wouldn't. I left the state I was in and went someplace else; a place I liked and one that felt good to me. So yes, I was irritable and unruly when I couldn't get to go there or my booze ran out.

I was placed in Athens because it seemed that I drank more and more to reach that level. Also it seemed that the level line I sought for continually seemed to raise itself. So when the sheriff found me they thought I was a nut, retarded or something. I only crapped myself and was in a semi coma, nothing too bad. Nonetheless I was sent to Athens to dry out and man was that a trip. The times I had to live without my liquor my body rebelled with ferocity and I was tied to a bed for 3 days by my hands, feet and arms. They only propped me to feed me like soup broth or some crap like that, so in doing so, yes you guessed it, I didn't crap, but I did pee all over that damn bed and myself. They did not dare leave me untied or I know I would have killed someone in order to be relieved of my sufferings. Late into the third day they did untie me but still had me locked up in a room by myself. This went on for 7 more days and the food was slid through a slot in the door. Then I was able to come out and visit all my cell buddies. Damn I tell you that place could make you crazy. People are something else. I needed to stay away from them and try to keep my head straight. I wanted out and didn't know if I wanted to get better or not, but I did know that I wanted out.

I used to spend a lot of time looking out of the window and I found a small bracket support on my bed frame that was propped lose on one side and I only had to spend a short time on relieving it from the frame. It was about 1/8" thick by about 1/2" and about 6" long. So that is what I used to scratch those words on the stone. Listen, do you want to know what it was like in there… I will tell you. I was on the second level of crazies because I was violent without my drink. But listen how stupid this all was. The guys next to me if they started showing out the attendants would give them laudanum, which is like a drink or shot of whiskey, to help them calm down. When I would show out and want to calm down them fuckers would tie me up, put me in a room and tell me to deal with it. What the hell is this? I really thought if you were mildly screwed up they would surely help you the rest of the way in that place. Anyway, I was able to control myself and after 4 months I was able to leave and boy did I ever! I went straight to Athens got me a bottle, drank it and shared none. I then didn't want to be close to that hill again and caught me a ride to Ironton and that is where I settled down. I got drunk as much as I could and finally ended up with syphilis. I then got myself cut in two big pieces cause that's what happens to a feller that passes out in a set of rail tracks. Nope, I wasn't crazy – never was. Yes, I was stupid for some things like getting syphilis, getting in a knife fight, stealing and a couple other stupid things, but mostly I was lonely and I was hurt from when I was a kid. Nope, never was crazy. Hey, want me to autograph that stone for you? Guess it's kinda famous now, eh? Nope I am not in the cemetery but some here thought you might like my story. I am not even really in this group either.

Marty

Emma (Emily) Jane (Gifford) Holsinger
1856-1911

Chapter Eleven

My name is Emma and this is my story. I was born in Meigs County and was the 3rd of eight children; a brother, a sister, I, another two sisters, another brother, and two more sisters. My younger brother David was killed when he was 7 years old. Our light carthorse kicked him in the back and snapped his neck, we think because he had no support to his head and died very soon after the occurrence. We were raised on a small hill farm and did what was needed to make any kind of a living. My older sister, my mother and I did mostly laundry for hire for sawmill hands nearby. We also raised some small vegetables and eggs that we peddled. My dad and brother worked hauling lumber for the mill mostly to the rail yards. After my brother was killed, my mother was never the same. Her little boy was very special to her and although it really wasn't anyone's fault, my dad made mother believe she was neglectful and was at fault. From then on mother became very agitated. She worried about everything and focused on little things. She would worry herself into exhaustion and would need to be in bed for weeks. It became quite sad since she would worry that bees would sting one of the little ones and they would die or a rat would bite and kill them as they slept. So mother would constantly check on the children. The smaller children felt much of the obsession, more so than the older ones, and our poor mother never forgave herself neither did our father.

I met a young traveler when I was 17 named John Holsinger and he too worked in the mills. Two months before I was 18 years old my father gave his consent for us to marry and we did. We then moved to Ross County then to Adams County. Our life together was mostly good. Work was hard and we had a small home we rented. John worked as a hired hand and farm labor. John was 3 years older than I and knew a lot of things. He was never mean or abusive to me, but he was firm and just. He never drank. He smoked a pipe occasionally. He liked sex and often had me do things for him, but he was very smart and when we finished he and I were both satisfied. Our first son was then born when I was 19 years old. I asked to name him David to honor my little brother that died so young. Things were fine until David began to walk, then our second child Emily was born and I had one sucking and one trying to walk. I became very worrisome over David as I kept imagining him falling down steps or into a well or something. My husband worked away. I then became pregnant again and now had two toddlers and a new one to feed. All of my emotions pilled higher and higher with each child. I increasingly had worry that one was going to die. Yes, I guess I was afraid that by my not watching over my flock that one would perish and I would be blamed just like my mother and I would live the rest of my life with the exact same guilt. By the time the last child was born I was thin, very thin, weak and fragile in my nerves and mind. I now became very much as my mother did and worried constantly about not providing well for my husband and children. I stopped sleeping and began to talk out loud and express my constant worry. I was obsessed; it consumed my every thought and me. On top of all of this my littlest babe Ruben was the smallest of all and I didn't have any milk to feed him nor the strength. John was able to get goat's milk from a neighbor and I believe it is all that saved Ruben from the jaws of death itself. I became trapped in my body. I sat and talked about how I was to care for and protect the children, how much flour was needed for the bread, when to bring in and take out the laundry, what windows to close at night to prevent chills and draft, where to go in a storm, how much to feed the baby and what size shoes the older ones needed, where the darning needles were kept, what should be preached about on Sunday, what hog should be butchered next, grandma's sauerkraut recipe and how much wood we would need for the winter months. I knew all of this, my mind knew this, but I was a prisoner in a body that simply would not move. I could talk and I spoke of all of the above often. All of those kinds of thoughts would flood my mind and would require that I not sleep.

John was a good man and that is why he felt it best to find me a place that could deal with me. He was so smart that he knew he would do the best thing for me. I believed that going to Athens meant that I would be helped to move my body again and not be trapped inside. I never believed that I was going to be left and that others would watch me without any help available. Shortly after arriving I realized that all of my hope was gone and that unless I could come out of my body I would be imprisoned the rest of my days. I began to worry again about my little ones and who would worry for them with me away. Now my plight was constant and I felt very little reason to continue on. All hope for me was gone and I believed this just as I believed that no one was caring for my babies since I was the only one to constantly worry for them. I had no contact with them and no visits either. Neither knowing about their care nor outcome, I found it difficult to bear it all, nor did I. I felt all I could do was to lay myself out and offer to die to end my misery. I truly thought I could, but after one or two days of laying on the floor I would be so weak that the staff would prop me up and force food and water into me and I would not perish on that day.

I, too, was part of the "Cottage Industry" for periods at a time, but it seemed to be off and on due to my bony frame. I was one that was led to a room and laid onto a bed and did not move as all I wanted to do was to die and so everything and anything could be done to my body without resistance as I hoped that this would help in my deliverance. My spells rose and fell in waves; I was fed even though I didn't want to eat my body would allow it and then when my body would lie down it behaved as if my insides did not agree and I was unable to stop it or move. This constant battle between my mind and my body kept me in a state of constant confusion. During these waves I gained and lost weight terribly. When I was very thin and bony nobody would desire my body, but when I would increase then I would once again lay out to die and wish for it only to find a strange man on me without being able to stop him. The constant up and down made my teeth a sore sight and many fell out as well as much of my hair, as it was quite thin. I had hardly any breasts and unless I was completely nude, you would generally have a hard time believing that I was really a woman and not a young boy or a stick for that matter.

That is my story. I talked fast and overlapped, as that was how the thoughts I had in my head were, but I was unable to carry out the simplest tasks of helping myself. I often wondered why my mind and body would not work together. I never stopped worrying for my children. I thought that I would like to kill myself but could not make my body respond to my requests. I only felt if I wanted to die enough, then I would. I often found myself lying on the floor and wishing to have it all end. I never saw my John or my children for the rest of my days and I did finally die and that was my end. I lay down and I believe that having gone through this so many times my mind and body finally found a way to be together.

Emma Holsinger
#321
1856-1911

I hope the children of the children of my children will read this story of mine and that somehow they will come to know how much I loved them and that although I couldn't show it, I felt it and never stopped worrying for them. I loved you all.

All my love,
Mom

Joseph Enochs
1829-1881

Chapter Twelve

Hello, I am Joe! I fought for the Union as did all young fellers my age, since it was our call of duty to do so. After the war was over however, I was injured and that is why I was at the asylum. We were all at the home place on a Saturday; dad, Uncle Joe, my brother and two cousins. The barn on dad's place needed new roofing, so we were replacing the whole roof. All new shingles had been split and the rafters were in good order. Dad and Uncle Joe felt the nail boards should be replaced. Most of the work was done and my cousins Clive and Lloyd were beginning to lay the shingles. My brother Thomas was aloft and finishing the nail boards. I was sending them up cut to length by way of a rope.

I sent a board up about 12 feet long as I had several times before, and as it was about to clear the eaves and be dragged into place the rope let go and down it came. I heard the yells of warning and saw it actually coming my way when I barely had time to raise my arms and partly turn to protect my head. The end of that board came down and hit me on the back part of my head and drove my head and face into the ground.

I broke some teeth and busted my face up. Blood came out of my ears on both sides and I couldn't seem to unclench my teeth. I went in and out of sleep for 2 or 3 days after that. When I finally woke up it seemed I was a totally different person. I was now left handed instead of right handed, I had constant pain in my head and neck that never seemed to go away and I had involuntary problems. My lower lip would just hang and made my communication slow and difficult. I limped on one side and my right hand seemed stiff and responded slowly. I couldn't seem to remember much at all of my growing up years.

I was told that my injury was severe and the damage would be long lasting. I had a scar on the back of my head from where the skin was split open. My mother and aunt sewed my head back together, but the skull was fractured and a rather large piece remained loose. Mother explained that it floated and when pushed upon, my brains would push it back up. So mother positioned it the best she could straight in its seat and pulled the skin back tight as she sewed me back together. It healed fine and I suffered no infection, but the effects were quite involved.

I always had a dent in the back of my head. After about a year it became hard again, but other things began to happen. I had a constant pain in my head that never ended even with sleep. I had spells where I would see two of everything in front of me. Sometimes everything would just go black, but after a short spell would come back again. My lower lip sagged and it was quite a challenge to drink a sip. I could still talk, but I was very hard to understand. I would stop in the middle of a thought and not continue again. Yes, I broke my jaw when I landed on the ground and it broke on the hinging part and it never healed all the way on my right side so it was often painful to eat or move my mouth. The other odd thing was that it was as if I was looking at someone else's arm whenever I tried to move my own, based on the fact that my arm never responded. I could not make my arm move from my shoulder down. It just hung by my side and made no movements by my willing.

After one year and six months I was out and about and eager to help around the farm. I had so many limitations that I was no longer able to dress, feed, nor clean myself. Although my mother wished to care for me, she was completely burdened by the care of dad's mother and was not up to the added labor of my care as well. So the idea was presented to admit me to the asylum for the insane in Athens. Although nobody believed I was insane, they were told that this place was a caring place and aspiring to a hospital as well, therefore better prepared to care for the needs of a person like myself.

The pain in my head only grew worse and my arm hung, but seemed to start to twitch occasionally at the shoulder joint. It still would not respond, but it did move some. The times that my eyes would go black became more frequent and lasted for longer periods. My neck became stiff over the years to follow and prevented me from turning my head to the right. I was not treated poorly at the asylum, though I was lumped in with the simple- minded. I was totally dependent on another person to wash me, clean me after a crap, dress and often feed me. The worst part was waiting until someone felt like feeding me when I was half starved, although I could still use my left hand. My jaw would sear with pain and it was difficult to keep food in my mouth since my lip and face were numb.

I died at the asylum and my dad died before me. Although I was not really that far from home, it was still quite a trip. So after dad died, I felt I was quite forgotten. I realize that my brother and mother would have liked to have me home to bury, but notice of my departure never reached my family and I believe had they known, I would have been sent for. I remain in the cemetery. I mustered in the service in Ross County in 1861. My commanding officer was Milo Talbott in the 5^{Th} Ohio Light Infantry. I was never wounded in the body but in the mind. I was mustered out of service in 1865.

Joseph Enochs
#78
1821-1881

Elizabeth Walker
1821–1891

Chapter Thirteen

Hello, I am Elizabeth Walker. I was known by most as "Lizzie." I was married in 1840 to a fine man named Johanas Walker and we lived all of our married life in Ohio. Johanas went through the war, as did every other able body it seemed, and came home to me on a July day in 1865. He rarely carried a gun being part of a signal corps, although he saw much action. His experiences affected him to be sure, but he saw things mostly in his sleep that troubled him again.

My account details the events around September of 1871. Johanas and I were never blessed with children. Our desires for them were strong, but perhaps Our Lord God knew that our home would not be fit for young ones. Our closest neighbor, DJ Lanner, was about a mile up the lane. He had a lumber mill and Johanas worked with him more than a hired hand, but not quite as a full partner. His portion of the millwork was enough for us to live right with his investment of $71.00.

Johanas was working the tailing of the lumber as usual on a September day. His handiness and strength allowed him to work nearly all day at a tremendous speed. On that day though, I didn't know that I would never hear him say another word to me again. As he had done many times before, he worked as close to the blade as he needed to, but in this one incident Johanas stumbled just enough to trip himself too close to the blade as even at the idle speed it was able to grab his shirt sleeve and pull him into its path. DJ was able to shut down the mill fast enough, but regardless Johanas was practically cut in half.

The boys went two ways; one to fetch the surgeon and the other to come my way. I was able to hear the steam whistle call of concern as well as the boy's cry as he was still about 100 acres away. I arrived soon after he was freed from the blade and he was carried to the house and laid on the table. The sights were quite startling and the impressions were permanently fixed to my memory. Johanas was open-eyed most of the time. His left arm was held to him only by skin and a small stretch of meat, which the surgeon quickly relieved him of. The side of his chest was openly exposed as his ribs were very visible as well as some of the inner workings of his upper chest. Blood was abundant, but not overly for some reason. The gap in his skin was quite an opening and the wound was, for the most part, quite clean sparing a few wood chips.

The surgeon did his best to pull my Johanas' chest closed with a needle and thread. This remedy was very crude and for the most part quite ineffective. He was bound and held together with strips of cloth. Johanas opened his eyes often. His lips moved as if trying to speak though no sound was to be heard. He blinked rapidly and swallowed often, but mostly laid still. His bindings soaked through in less than an hour's time and were changed on the hour except at night when it was done twice per night. The new dressings were coated with clear bacon grease and a salve of comfrey. Each new dressing allowed the startling sight of Johanas' innards moving to sear my vision and added to my thoughts of helplessness.

My poor Johanas never ate another meal and tried to drink from a wetted cloth, but basically faded from me. We sat with him for three days and two nights only to see him quietly slip from us into a continuous sleep never to wake again. As we watched the movements of breath that came to us without our knowing, he seemed to leave us in the same manner. My beloved Johanas was buried on our small sixteen-acre farm in Adams County, Ohio in September of 1871 and that was when my story began, if you will.

For the next three months I relived the accident of my Johanas over and over again in my mind. Although I wasn't actually there at the time, I heard the saw, I saw the blood, heard the flesh being sawed, I felt the commotions and I focused on the grotesque sight of my man's insides moving inside of his chest over and over and over again. Some nights the scene played as many as a dozen times, each one as vivid and each haunting detail just as sharp as the last. This daily occurrence slipped me into exhaustion to the point of being unable to raise my head.

DJ's wife and daughter were kind to me as were a few other neighbors, but were rarely able to offer me the comfort I needed. At times I got up, took care of my personal needs and even fed the cats, but something like a speck on the porch that resembled a piece of saw dust we removed from Johanas' wound brought all of the gory details flooding back once again. In the spring my sister Molly came to stay a spell to help with affairs and saw to my recovery. She was a tremendous help and it seemed that she occupied me enough in the garden or even with a walk to the barn. My visions overcame me in my sleep and I slept very little. I often avoided sleep for long periods of time for fear of the chance of reliving my frights. After a period of doing this, I collapsed into a near comatose state and slept for two days in a row.

When it became apparent that the wound in my mind would not heal and was too large, just as Johanas' was, Molly thought it best for everyone to seek the help of the home for the insane in Athens. I was at the asylum for four years and in that time I cried often. I lamented and I refused myself sleep for long periods. I did not like to be touched and fought or screamed when someone did so. I was used in the house of prostitution occasionally, but due to my violent fits when someone touched me, it seemed not to be worth the involved process for the bindings it took to restrain me in order for my body to be of any comfort to a man and after four visits to the "Cottage M" I was basically left alone. My death came upon me as they thought I was malnourished, but in actuality my heart failed and allowed me to be free from my inner torturing.

Mrs. Elizabeth Walker / "Lizzie"
99
1821-1891

Mary Channey
1859-1899

Chapter Fourteen

My name is Mary and my story begins in 1889 in Chillicothe, Ohio where I lived with my husband Wyatt and our two children. Wyatt and I married 6 years earlier and our married life was mostly a normal one. He worked for the city preparing roads and making new ones. He was involved in many tasks working for the city and could do almost any kind of work; sidewalks, curbs, steps, planting, but mostly he worked on the roads. Then he hurt his back and was laid at home for almost a month. When he was able to get about again he hadn't the strength he once had and the work that was at hand was not work that he was able to do, so he was not called back to work. Bad times came around us as our bills were still with us but the ways to pay them were not. After four months Wyatt was able to find work separate from small odd jobs with the rail yard where he worked with friends connecting or stacking train loads. Money started to come to us again, but as we were behind a great deal it was a slow process to catch up. With a small jingle in his pocket, his friends persuaded him to attend fights with them and turn the small coins into paper money. This was all a chance and a risky one as well. Some winnings were made but as they were made larger bets were placed and larger losses were also at hand. I found out later that fights were not all he would spend on, but cards and animal fights as well, anything to change his coins into large piles without having to work for it.

Although money was being made at the rail yard and some bills were being paid our home was still sparse. We lived in a small upper floor next to a grain loading elevator. It was not bad. It was noisy during the day and due to the dust I was unable to open windows until evening to cool things down. This was somewhat hard on the little ones, Martha was 3 years old and Davis was a year old. So much of the day would be spent out doors to stay cool. Wyatt's obsession with trying to turn one dollar into a million overnight became just that, an obsession, and the money we had to live on was increasingly smaller amounts only due to the fact that he was gambling and losing more and more. This was all unbeknownst to me until I was made aware. I noticed many things happening with Wyatt; like his temper and lack of involvement with the children. He was never abusive, he only yelled a lot it seemed at silly little things and would stay away at night with friends. I wondered if all wives had this set up where their man left at 5 a.m., worked all day, came home to change his shirt and left again only to return after midnight. I wondered if Adam did this to Eve and if this was all there was and all I had to look forward to.

As things continued to spiral downward in our home Wyatt came home less and less. One evening in the fall it was past midnight when a caller came to the door. Wyatt was asleep in the chair and went to the door only to let 3 men in our front room. The talk was loud and chairs were moving about and I was afraid the little ones would be awakened. As I put on my wrap and went to the front room I noticed Wyatt at the table with a man behind him holding his hair and a large knife sticking in the table before him and tears in Wyatt's eyes. As I entered the room a man was behind the door I guess as I too was grabbed by the hair and made to sit across from Wyatt at the table. This is where I found out that Wyatt was making very good money and betting very big and losing very big. Much money was lost and much money was owed; almost $300 which we did not have and these men wanted now. Wyatt kept trying to settle with them and was getting nowhere. That is when an agreement was met for one week to come up with $150.00 and the remainder in the second week. All agreed and then as the man doing the talking came up with the idea that just to be sure that Wyatt would not forget and that there would be in fact an interest on his debt, he decided that I would be the one to pay the interest. That is when the man holding me pushed me onto the table, lifted my night gown and took full liberties with my body in full view of my husband. When he was finished I was offered to the second man but he declined. I was left to clean myself and go back to bed and I chose to sleep with the children as Wyatt left for the night.

    The week went by and we only saw Wyatt one evening as he came to change but was mostly not around. Then the time came when the money was owed and I was certain that Wyatt had learned a very valuable lesson and had met his obligation. I was wrong because just having fed the children in the evening, again the same 3 men showed up at the door to collect the money and Wyatt was not at home. Having no money, no answers nor able to offer Wyatt's whereabouts I was dragged to the bedroom by one of the men and told to take off my dress. He was very violent and hit me about the face often, he said so that Wyatt would remember his responsibilities. He raped me repeatedly and left me on the rug beside the bed. As he left the man who talked mostly came in and closed the door. He took me by the hair and took me to the window then made me stick my hand on the window ledge and had all intentions of crushing my hand in the window. As he dropped the window I moved my hand forward just enough for the impact to hit my arm just above the wrist. He was very angry and knowing that he did not create the damage he intended he raised the window and slammed it two more times and did finally crush my arm. He then just left and was laughing as he left mentioning that they would be back in one week for their money. I was afraid for the children so we left for my sister's house across town. Julia and her husband were very kind. My arm was looked at and although it was not crushed one bone was broken and it was pulled into line and wrapped tightly in order for it to heal. Wyatt came home to collect some belongings and then as he wanted no more of this to befall myself nor the children he agreed to leave town and let them know he was doing so. The children and I stayed with Julia and her husband.

We would see Wyatt off and on for the next two years but we never knew when he would come by. He sent Julia money and at times somewhat large amounts. I knew he must still be betting but with this money on hand he had to have paid his bill to the three men.

After two and a half years Wyatt strolled back into town with a new suit and wanting a new start. He said he was a new man and all his debts were paid and he wanted his family again. Although he didn't have a job, he said he was looking for work and had a small chunk of money to see us through until he could do so. We were able to move out and into a slightly bigger house on the other side of town not very far from the elevator again. The children had a difficult time to get to know their father again and life although quiet was still strained.

I began having nightmares the moment Wyatt came back and they were very often it seemed. Wyatt did find work with the newspaper and at a bar at night. We lived for a few years as married strangers, all the while Wyatt was still doing his betting and would only actually work the bar occasionally, mostly betting. Again our lives were on a slow downward progression and Wyatt was slipping back into his old losing habits. I kept having dreams of the rape and abuse and Wyatt would not sleep with me or even in the same room. Mostly he felt guilt about what happened and partly because I lost my desire to be touched as a woman.

To speed along this account I will tell you this; Wyatt took us to the place of being in debt again and owing the same people as before and I had no way of knowing this until one evening they broke down the door again. Determined to defend myself this time I kept a small skinning knife beside the bed under the cloth, but I was not anywhere near it. The scene was all too familiar as the same dialogue was present; you owe us money, Wyatt's pleading and begging for time and mercy, the children's cries as they were beside the table, the talk of a deadline and the interest that would be taken out on my body. Again I was dragged to the bedroom by my hair and my hands bound behind me. When the door opened Wyatt was placed in a chair and made to watch the whole thing. I was laid across the bed with my dress up and the men all behind me talking about very bad things they would and wanted to do to me without actually touching me. This went on for almost an hour. Then one man actually did take my body and I was left. Wyatt was beaten severely. As the men left one stroked the hair of my 12 year old and said that maybe tomorrow he would have both of us.

I took the children to my parents' farm near Hallsville and left them. Wyatt was badly beaten and went to the hospital for treatment. I went back to the house to gather only things such as clothes, photos and a set of dishes. It was around noon and again I was caught alone by the same three men. I was tied fully nude in a chair and left for almost two hours. My mouth was gagged so there was no way to call out. The men would visit as they waited for Wyatt. I told them he was so badly beaten that it was unlikely he would return. Bad things were discussed regarding how to disfigure me or how to get money out of me for long periods of time. I was again raped by all three this time and for a long time, almost until evening. I was then beaten in the face and I remember only one hit that was very hard to the side of my head and then I remember nothing more.

I awoke at a nearby hospital ward and was mostly covered with bandages. Many people asked for an account of what took place and who was responsible. I was unable to give my account as I only spoke in confusion. I can see now why I behaved as I did then, but while I was experiencing it, I was completely incoherent. I was haunted at night of visions of horrible sights. I was haunted by day of any male coming near me and I could not even form a sentence. I was looked after by a physician and recommended to go to the asylum to heal. I understand that Wyatt was summoned to sign my order. The children stayed with my parents for a while but eventually went to Julia's house and she raised them for me. While at the asylum I was a troublesome patient and although the intention was for a healing I never did get better as my wounds were deep and unable to be healed.

I was a handful and I was crazy. I had only mostly lost my mind.

Anytime I saw a male I tore my clothes completely away from my body, ran up to them, turned around and bent over. In my mind I knew they would eventually get to this anyway and if I saw them talking they would only be talking about the horrible things they were going to do to me. In many ways the waiting was much harder to accept than the actual act, so I was merely trying to get it over with.

I was at the asylum for two years and in that time my mother, father, my two children and my sister (but not her husband) would visit on a very regular schedule, mostly every other month. I was not mistreated at the asylum, but it was of the utmost importance that no one ever touched me. I died of pneumonia in 1899 after a long winter of congestion.

Due to the nature of my abuse along with the extent, I chose not to include all of the details. My experience happened and there is nothing neither you nor I can do to change that. Ignoring it does not cease its existence.

I found out later that Wyatt was found dead hanging by his neck. All believed that he took his own life, as he should have.

Mary Chaney
1859-1899

Mary Sprouse
1846-1908

Chapter Fifteen

Hello my name is Mary. My name was Mary Sprouse, not Spoonce. I am not sure how the mix-up happened with the grave recorders, but perhaps poor penmanship can be to blame. It seems that much of my experience was harsh and hard also. I grew up fast and being the 3rd girl of 8 children I was made to hold responsibilities fast. I was introduced and encouraged into the field of "ladies' work" when I was 16. My two older sisters were of the vocation as well and our father did the booking and held our finances. It seems that it was the only thing I did well with myself and it didn't take a lot of skill to spread your legs.

Let me tell you about the dumb ass at the admittance board that laughed when I told them I was at Lincoln's assassination. Why do you think that would be so funny? And why is it so unbelievable? I must admit that I was not at the actual shooting itself as only very high paid whores were allowed to enter the theatres, but directly across from the theatre and on the next block was a house of rooms. I happened to be entertaining all week leading up to the show and I happened to be doing the very same thing when all of the commotion in the street began. Although I did get paid in advance my client was cut short on his visit. I was 29 years old at the time and a very full figured woman. It was a sad time following Abe's death and work was slow. I went to Pittsburg to stay with some friends for a short stay.

The risks were great in this profession. They included; disease, beatings and pregnancy. The worst being pregnancy! Why? Because after a hard beating you could be back at it in a day or two and when the lights were low they were not inspecting your body and the bruises weren't that noticeable. Most of the nasty diseases had you down for a month at most, but even with that I still had my mouth to help make a living, but with a pregnancy, that was different and the down time either way was longer than was handy.

You think I would have learned. I was pregnant 13 times and let 8 of them go to full term. So I had a lot of down time. Some girls I ran with would only allow it in the bum to avoid these side effects, but when things get heated up it's hard to keep to those rules and well, you know what happens. Most of the babies went with my mother and some to an aunt. Three went to homes for kids because I was never ever cut out to be a mother. I married four times in my life. One only lasted a week and the last one was to Wilbur Sprouse. We were married eight years and I had two children that my Aunt gave back when she became too old and they were about 11 and 13.

When I became 58 years old I started to act strangely and events would slip by me. As the years went by I became worse, so much so that Wilbur had me sent to the asylum in Athens to protect me from myself he'd say. I suffered from old lady whore disease! I just crapped out in my mind. Things ran together in my head and ran out of my mouth in that same mixed up order. So although all of the events were true and facts were true, once they were lumped together nobody believed any of them and you were told you were nuts!

What's so hard about believing that I was 35 years old and I was there when Lincoln was shot in McArthur, Ohio? Again, all of this was true it's just that I was 35 years old 25 years ago! I was at Lincoln's assassination giving a blow job! I was in McArthur, Ohio living with my third husband and making two children. So what was so hard about believing that and is that enough to put me away? I was in the Madame industry of "Cottage M" but only for about six months as a 60-61 year old that was of such full plumpness and sagginess. They told me I was "undesirable." Now figure this; some girls would be dragged there screaming, had to be beaten and tied and here stood a well seasoned beauty willing to walk on over and they said I was undesirable! Figure that! Well hell, turn off the lights and they'll never know! Ah, just as well the way my mind was going, I'd probably forget how to do it soon anyway! So that's about it. I died of a bad cold/flu. I got fluid in my lungs and croaked. It wasn't so bad at the asylum except for the real fruits. Now they were scary to me, but I stayed on the lower levels of insanity and stayed to myself.

That's about it – my life didn't amount to much other than I did bring a smile to a great number of men's faces throughout my stay. I was a lousy mother and wife.

Mary Sprouse
#290
1846-1908

John Doe #2 - David Edward (Eddy) Littmar – "Jub"
1858-1910

Chapter Sixteen

Hello, I am Eddie! I am part of this group. We call ourselves and we are referred to as Ted's Group. There are a bunch of us here and as I look around I realize that everyone has a story to tell. So you wonder why you are going to hear my stupid story? It is because I was chosen. That's right. A small group of people got together and I realized that not all stories could be recorded yet and so a bit of a lottery had to take place. Of course, Ted is the one organizing all of this so that is how I was chosen. Quite random, as would it have been for interesting content, I would have been dropped from the list for sure.

A good thing to openly discover is that the asylum didn't actually help a great number of people. In fact it was not much more than a containment center where people just stayed and were contained in a small area so as to not burden, embarrass or harm normal society. This work is a great challenge for mankind to explore their inner feelings and judgments they still have pertaining to the mentally ill. Also the fact that so many real people are in their final resting spot anonymously is tragic in itself. The basic right thing to do is to at least put their names on the headstones – kind of a period at the end of a sentence. You would feel a great discomfort leaving a sentence or a thought without a period wouldn't you? Same thing here – it is not the myth that families were ashamed of having names on stones! It is clear plain old laziness and lack of respect. All of the people here were never respected and it is quite evident in just the fact that nobody took the small amount of time to put our names out there.

You know the family embarrassment that is spoken of right? Like everyone comes to that simple little cemetery with a notepad and keeps track of all the Thomases that were buried there and goes clear back to Adams or Knox County and tells everyone!!!! For crying out loud! They never came to visit when they were living – what's going to make anyone want to come and spend an afternoon in an old cemetery? This is so much needed for those full of compassion, for us and what we experienced. It is for the families that accept what is what and want to go on. This is to do what is plain old right.

My name is Eddie - that is what I was called. Although my start out was quite difficult my given name at the time I popped out was David Edward Littmar. My mamma was only 16 years old and the year was 1858. My mamma's name was Anita Littmar, my father was Robert Littmar. He was my father, my uncle and mamma's brother. Crappy, I know, but he had been raping mamma for 3 or 4 years and she became pregnant when she was only 15. She lived in Meigs County, Ohio and as all of these stories were a shame and a disgrace to her family, she was allowed to stay at home throughout her pregnancy, but was never allowed to be in sight of any visitors. Then it came time for me to see a sunrise. Her daddy said she couldn't have the baby at home and so I was born at a neighbor's house above a corn crib on a September afternoon.

My mamma was so glad to see me and although I had all the things a little boy should when he is born and the right number of them, I wasn't and wouldn't ever be "right." I was made too close and I was what you would call "inbred!" God didn't intend for this to work, but it's the result of man's lust and ignorance. Mamma knew when I was only 2 or 3 years old that things were not right with me. Having never had a little one of her own to raise, she wasn't quite sure how and how fast things were supposed to happen with a baby. I was a happy baby but I didn't even start to walk until I was about 5 years old. I was still in diaper rags until I was 10 and I just wasn't right in my thinking. So many things were wrong; I was cross-eyed and couldn't focus on one thing like someone talking to me. I moved my eyes around constantly. I never learned to communicate. I grunted or moaned when I wanted something and if nobody listened, I grunted with a steady higher and higher pitch until someone noticed me. Mamma and I were allowed to go back home and we lived on a little bitty farm with my grandparents. Grandma was the most kind to me as she just plain had pity on me. My mamma was always good to me and did her best. Grandpa couldn't forgive her for being a trashy little slut that got knocked up and this was her penance for it. He never knew that his trashy little horny son was my daddy and Mamma never did tell him either. Uncle daddy Robert ended up going to Morgantown, West Virginia to work in the coal and that was that.

Mamma ended up finally meeting a nice man named Dale Starner when she became 28 years old. They got married and had two more children; my brother and sister. Dale worked for the railroad and we all lived happy. Dale was away a lot as he built or repaired railroads, but things were nice when he was home. He wasn't always the best with me, but he was kind for sure. My story seems long especially for such a boring one, but what happened is my brother and sister grew up to be fine people and left us at home. Daddy got killed by some men who jumped him and some others on the rail line and it left me and mamma at home alone. Mamma got railroad pension money and we lived together for a long time. I was 39 years old when Mamma went to heaven and my brother and sister never did come to the funeral since I didn't know how to find them to tell them and nobody else did either. So me, a preacher man, the sheriff and two men with shovels sent Mamma on her way. That is when I was sent to the insane asylum. I had great needs to be sure, but Mamma knew me and I knew her and we took good care of each other, but nobody was around to take care of "Eddie" now so I had to go away.

I got really scared when Mamma wasn't around anymore and I couldn't talk to nobody and nobody understood me. I would get real nervous around people and I would suck and bite on my bottom lip so hard that blood would run down my chin. I always carried a cloth with me, like a great big handkerchief. When I would get excited and bleed Mamma would have me bite on that rag instead of my lip. When I went to the asylum they took my rag and it wasn't for a very long time until I got another one to replace it. I think it was actually a part of my under shorts!

I didn't act or respond well. I was often frustrated and for some reason I needed to be reminded of everything all of the time; like to remember to lower my pants to go to toilet, or that I needed to eat, or when it was dark I had to sleep, and occasionally I would need to take all of my clothes off and wash my body! If you would tell me today to do these things I could make it through the night, but come morning I had no idea what to do. Mamma always did these things and reminded me. So finally after about a year and some months the attendants were able to put and keep me on a regular schedule and I knew when to do the everyday things that I needed to do. When I was at the asylum nobody ever knew my name Mamma gave me because nobody ever told them. Somehow I got the name "Jub" and that's what everyone called me for 14 years. I lay down and died - a blood vessel got real big and busted in my head and I died when I was almost ready to go to sleep.

David Edward Littmar
"Jub"
#459
1910

Eliza (Fe La Quois) Smith
1869-1935

Chapter Seventeen

Hello to you all. My name is Eliza Smith. I was born in the year of 1869 in Baton Rouge, Louisiana. My daddy's name was Fe La Quois, he did plaster work. My brothers, sisters and I were the first generation to be born free Fe La Quois. Free is not really for those with dark skin, so although we were not officially slaves, there wasn't a whole lot of difference in our daily life.

As I grew up I took on work, working for mostly white folks around about Louisiana and Mississippi. I cooked a lot as that is what I learned most. I met a tall young man named Calvin Smith visiting from Georgia. We fell in love and were married. We moved to Ohio because word was received about the Quaker People helping black families obtain small pieces of land to own and farm. Once I heard this, I knew I just had to go see this Ohio farm ground.

We settled in Chesterhill, Ohio and thought we were in heaven. The Promised Land was before us now and we were settled on a piece of it.

The Quakers were very helpful. The truth about the land was not all quite what was told to us, but Calvin and I were able to have a small piece of land, about 6 acres. We could live there for free if we agreed to clear it, dig a well and put up a house the first year. All of the money from the crops was ours to keep and in five years we had the option of buying the six acres if we wanted to stay. So we started to work and hard work it was. We cleared a spot for the house, dug the well and began building the foundation of the house.

Neighbors and friends helped us put out our first crops and in July we had some cultivating to do, but most of the time work was spent on the house. We gathered all of the stone we could from the fields. The stones were not that nice and much more were needed for the chimney. Our house was only 18' X 24', with one room in a 1½ story log house. Calvin was able to borrow the mule and stone boat from the neighbour and made many trips to the creek for stone. I was mostly right with him as the stones were fine and not too big for me to handle.

I had to push Calvin as he was a hard worker once he got moving, but getting him moving was a trick sometimes. Working by himself was hard for him, but off he went. He came back with two boat loads of fine stone and on the third load he was a bit late getting in. Soon I saw him coming in and later found out that he got snake bit. He cut the strike and bled it out, but not enough as he was already light in his head and staggering. I watched him fall against a tree and I called out to get help. The next few days found him getting plenty of fitful sleep and fever. We cut the strike again and let it bleed more. We put coal oil on it to help draw out the poison. His leg swelled up to twice the size of normal and it looked like the skin wouldn't stay around it anymore. He seemed to lock his jaws and we had the most dreadful time to get water in him. His lips cracked and the sores around his mouth looked quite uncomfortable. He swelled up his hip and up to his ribs and then it looked as if it would stop and go the other way only to see the swelling jump up to under his arm. His leg turned awful black and after four days Calvin had a fit that took his life and part of mine with him.

We buried him on the edge of our plot and not being able to keep up our end of our agreement on my own I had to leave. I stayed with friends some, but realized soon that I was an unexpected burden. I heard there was work offered to people like me with my skills in Zanesville, Ohio. That is where my troubles began. I started to feel guilty about what happened to Calvin and felt that it was my fault that I was now having to go back to being a cook or a house negro. It was me that pushed Calvin into the farming life as the prospect of being a land owner was so alluring. It was me that made him get up and get moving and me that pushed him so much to work on the house. It was me that had him fetching stones in the creek the day he got snake bit.

It seemed that these thoughts got bigger and bigger and louder with me. It seemed that if I went anywhere that people would be talking about me saying, "Oh, that's her there" or "Oh, that's the woman that got her man snake bit" and many other terrible things. Everywhere I went people were talking about me and how terrible I was. I found short term work in Zanesville, and heard that a cook was wanted up in Gallia County from some friends, so I went there. Nobody would know me and I would be free to move on and put my past behind. It was only about two months while working in a huge kitchen that I felt people talking about me again and, "what a no count nigger woman I was to let my man get snake bit and die." After a while, I started to agree with the words I heard and believed them. I thought I should be dead also. It got so bad that I did not sleep much and I did not work either. That was when the lady of the house called for her doctor to look at me and he determined that I was schizophrenic and I would benefit greatly from going to the new insane hospital in Athens. There I would get help to stop the beliefs and voices I heard. He said that they would be able to make everyone stop talking so bad about me. So I went and another story started there.

I was admitted to the Athens Lunatic Asylum in 1906 and was 37 years old. I was in the lower level degree of insanity. It wasn't that I was a threat to anyone, only to myself. I was watched closely most of the time.

Though my symptoms continued to grow and gradually got worse, I would sit for long times as I did not recognize the voices in my head nor did I invite them, but when twenty four hours of a voice that put me down as no good or no count then began to tell me, "you should die," I just jumped up and wanted to scream. I moved up the levels to 2 and I wanted more than anything to stop the voices. It seemed that nothing brought me relief.

Cottage "M" / Crazy Cat House

Sedatives calmed me to where, although I still heard voices and harmful ones, I just did not care as much, but they never did stop.

I, too, was involved in "Cottage M." If you need to know, everyone I knew of was involved. Only the violent crazies were not allowed. Some would act crazy violent, but their act was figured out and if they were young and firm they would just get tied up anyway. I was used there for a good many years and this is a very interesting fact; in all of my years there, I was only humped by one black man. Most of the men were short and overweight and almost all of them liked me on my hands and knees like a dog. It is my feeling that society would not allow them to poke a black woman like me, so they did me where nobody could see and nobody would tell. Only one man ever decided he was going to hurt me and he tried, but I grabbed his hand that was holding a belt and bent it back and I heard two of his fingers break. If someone had not come in at that moment, I would have broken them fingers clean off and when I was through there I was going after his man parts. I would have broken it off from the nuts and thrown it out the window! Hit me, will you? Ain't gonna happen, uh, uh, no way! So anyway, I never did mind walking to the "M Ward" as a funny thing would happen; while I was totally naked and had some fat, pale, white boy sweating on me, the voices would stop! Seriously! So in a way I kind of looked forward to a good poke and a bit of quiet along with that!

I had plenty of doctors that looked at me, all with fancy ideas too. I stayed in the second level mostly as sometimes the voices would get so loud and hurtful that I would want to bash my head on the wall and let them out. If it wasn't for the bars on my window cage, I would surely have flung myself out and dashed my brains on the road to end the constant torture.

I finally ran into a doctor that wanted to try some new cure for my destructive behavior and offered to help. He called it a Frontal Lobscopy, I think, not a lobotomy, but kind of the same. He placed me in a chair and strapped me in. I was tied up like a big black hog going to market. He gave me a lot of medicine that made me want to just give up. Then he put a small cut on the side of my head about where my temple is and then put a wooden handled thin ice pick tool beside my head and hit it with another hammer. He did this about six times to get it to push through my skull. I swear it was a good thing they thought to bolt down that chair to the floor as I surely would have upset it all. They gagged my mouth, but even so they said they heard me scream at the end of the hall. Once the pick was in, he angled it up between my eyes and started to move it back and forth, in and out, up and down. I still don't know why my eyes didn't pop out and roll down the hall! The idea was to scramble the front part of my brain or unhook it from the rest. He said that was the part that contained the voices. In about three minutes or so of this he drug the pick out, stuck gauze on the hole and put a wrap around my head. They couldn't untie me for more than an hour because my body was going crazy; jumping, twitching, etc. They tied my head back to the high back chair because it too was plain acting wild. When an hour passed my body quieted down and I realized that all the voices were gone! I realized that I had messed myself a couple of times and that my body completely stopped working. They cured me alright! I was now free of all the voices and I also was free of my body as it out right killed me! They called it a cerebral hemorrhage!

Well that is most of my story. I am not sure why the voices started with me nor why they wanted me to hurt me, but it did and they did and I tried. So once again you understand the importance of what is being done here. Everyone has a story to tell. It took time to get where we were, but it is the time getting there that was interesting. I am glad that it is so different here and I wouldn't go through that again for nothing.

Eliza Fe La Quois Smith
#624
1869-1935

Chapter Eighteen

Hello, my name is Samuel D. Wallace. I am a physician and would like to offer my insight pertaining to the Athens Insane Asylum. I was connected to your story and I hope my account will be of some benefit in helping to understand what took place and why.

During the War Between the States I was a surgeon's assistant who was but 2 years from finishing my studies to become a physician so I enlisted into the Northern Medical Corp. and felt that my "in the field training/hands on experience" would lend itself greatly to the intricate understanding of the human body. My field experience did very little to help my understanding but formed a tremendous amount of questions instead. When first arriving we did only one day, if that, of training. I had most of 2 years of official training, although there were many assistants that hadn't that and had never seen the inside of a man before.

I found my training up to this point had aided in my ability to understand or catch on and be of some earthly use. It was shortly after that that we were assigned to a surgeon and a field corp. was established. We were broken up into small groups for which we were all expected to carry out our responsibilities and in doing so would have an effective mobile surgical center.

As we moved our hospital ever close to the battle lines the casualties became more abundant, more severe and fresher. I mean that in the past should the severely wounded need to be transported to the field hospitals at a greater distance they very simply wouldn't make it and we wouldn't experience these kinds of wounds. So as we moved closer to the battles the wounds were in fact more severe and warranted the more rapid response from us in order to help the life not spill from the wounds. This was a totally different kind of doctoring than was taught to me in Medical School.

Some interesting things to note were the experiences we were running into on the front: perhaps a limb would be wounded by a bullet or saber's slash. Let's follow the wound created by a bullet for a moment. Usually a 58 caliber bullet hitting a limb directly would create a huge amount of damage. Let's also suppose that the bullet never exited the limb and is still lodged inside. The damage you would mostly notice is a likelihood of infection from gunpowder on the bullet and dirt in the wound from the falling or grabbing of the wound. Inside you generally would experience a large amount of bone fragments and finally the tearing and inflammation of tissue. So, what to do? Choices are to take the next hour to surgically remove the bullet and all surrounding bone fragments then sew the torn tissue back in place after immobilizing the limb to aid in the correct healing of the bone. Then depending on the entrance, you would leave it open so that the wound would drain itself as it began to heal. Now this is the best approach for this incident and most likely the best; securing this one wound could take 1-2 hours to effectively accomplish. When all of this was complete the wound would need to be cleaned and protected from dirt and flies regularly. Now knowing all of this and realizing that our surgical team could effectively and efficiently help perhaps 10-12 bullet-wound victims in a full day, how could this ever be followed? Consider that in one battle as many as 4-6 separate hospitals would be established and I recall one time when as many as 400 men lay in the shade of trees waiting to enter our tent only. Do we then go through and pick out the 12 men that we choose to survive? Not likely. It is once again when ideals are left and the practicality of nature is accepted as the rule and is then followed.

An entirely new approach was determined and adhered to. That was called amputation. At that point all wounds or extremities that were bullet related were generally and mostly amputated to the nearest joint above the wound. This would take perhaps 2-4 minutes. The large artery we called the bleeder would be pulled out and tied off and left long. Then the wound would be washed the best we could. The skin flap was quickly sewn over the stump and left loosely to drain on an edge, then adding a cloth wrap. This entire procedure could take as long as 15 minutes. Keeping in mind that the surgeon is only cutting and tying the bleeder as other assistants like myself would sew, wrap and prep.

Now we could effectively help 150-200 men wounded using this approach instead of 10. The remarkable thing was as crude a course of action as this was it was in fact a quite effective response to the account before us.

Now having said all of this quite windy account of life on the battle field I began to have more questions. I became intrigued at the resilience of the human body and as I retained images and thoughts my education in fact was still in progress.

I began to become intrigued by the driving force that would keep this body moving and reacting. Now I understood about the soul and when the spark of life leaves nothing more can be done. At least I thought I understood that, but perhaps what I did know about that was too limited. I wondered, when a man lay before me with the most unspeakable wounds your imagination could create, what would make this man continue to move and fight? I had been made to believe it was his heart! I disagreed because the heart is nothing more than a muscle that is reactionary to the whole. Take the blood from it or limit it and the heart would soon quit. So I believed it was something more, something much more involved and grand. It was then I realized that it must be the mind and I again realized how little I knew.

I once saw a man that was literally blown in half. His body was severed in two pieces. His right leg and thigh was held to him by his clothing and his left leg and thigh he dragged to keep close to him. He had no buttocks and genitals as they were gone and it was a full five minutes that he braced himself against a rock and continued to load and fire his weapon until he finally just accepted his circumstances and was overcome by his mortality.

This event and many others were the driving force behind the immense desire to want to know more about the complexities surrounding the human mind.

I often had to disassociate myself from the men we worked on. Although we were in fact saving men and giving them a chance to go home to loved ones, there were still rows of bodies of men that would never get that chance, even though we performed much of the same treatments. In keeping with all of this, I still had to view all of these patients not as men, but merely as cards stacked and all the same. In this manner, I was able to disconnect myself from the personal aspects of my calling. So here I was 35 years old and a field seasoned student again walking back into the Boston School of Medicine to finish my learning. Although I couldn't use much of the thoughts or procedures we adopted in the battle field hospitals, the insight it gave me was in fact quite helpful, but now a new way of thinking needed to take place. It was through my field service that the literal unquenchable hunger to delve into and understand the mind was created.

It was then I was introduced into the field of psychosis and the story of the clinically insane. This again is a very broad study as there are all levels and types of the insane. So I pursued a direction of trying to first understand what constituted one to be insane and then what it would take to treat this affliction.

That is how I eventually became associated with the Athens Asylum for the Insane. This was a grand new facility and it was a cutting edge study facility. I heard that there was a chance for a staff position and I sought for that employment. I was too late in obtaining the head position, but my training and desire was welcome and I served only as a visiting physician for the next three years.

Now the inside of the asylum, as you know, was quite involved and much of the medical protocol abounding on the battlefield was present there. There are times when simple practicality must be allowed to take over when the original guidelines are proven to be quite ineffective.

It was at this juncture in my career that I again realized how much I had thought I knew and compared that with how much I actually understood about mental illnesses.

I needed to try to separate those that were responding to life's conditioning from those who chose to cross the line of decency and were labeled criminally insane and still there were those that were in this capacity from birth. All were different and each unique with a battle wound, if only you could merely amputate just above the wound to isolate the chance of spreading an infection, thus resulting in healing. Unfortunately with mental illness a complex mystery is at hand as there are no apparent wound sites causing the affliction. There is basically no place to start. By the time they are admitted to the asylum they are in fact completely overrun by the spread of the infection.

So the choices and challenges began. We could just end the lives of those completely infected, but there are ethical concerns to remember. So take the ones that are not that bad and set them aside. Now concentrate on the newly infected and perhaps we could help cure them. This was a completely new method of treatment in medicine than was the physical I was exposed to earlier.

Everything was new and nothing was known for sure. Basically the patients in the asylum were in fact subjects to experiment on. Again you needed to disassociate yourself from each person to do this, because if you allowed yourself to realize that this subject was in fact someone's mother, father, daughter, etc. you personalized your feelings and accomplished very little.

There was much discussion among the medical professions and so many treatments were tried. A positive response was the goal and at times a difference was observed. Treatments that were barbaric at times were still practiced with results that varied extremely. Sometimes a positive alteration was noticed, but not often.

The drilling of the skull and removal of a disk of the skull to relieve the pressure on the brain was practiced hundreds of years earlier to let evil spirits out. It might have done that, but in my observation the hole must have been too small as the spirits chose to stay in.

Hydrotherapy was a new approach where the driving force behind it was to help shock the system back into its normal alignment. The theory was that if a shocking event took the mind in this direction perhaps another shock to the system would reverse its course and send it back again. Results were never much use and we in fact created full body burns and freezing of tissue, which created physical issues and did nothing for the mental aspects.

Laudanum was widely used by both patient and staff as a means to sedate and cope for both patient and attendant or attendant and attendee.

The jarring or jolting methods which were very rudimental and gruesome that were spoken about earlier were neither pleasant treatments nor effective either.

Basically I spent 3½ years working with the insane at Athens with very little progress into understanding or treating mental illness. I was a visiting physician and spent a fair amount of time traveling to other facilities and hospitals trying to understand more. I understood this: we knew nothing about the cause and cure of these people and the ironic thing about all of this is that even today the medical personnel know basically the same amount of nothing as we did pertaining to the disease we call mental illness. Modern medicine is used to postpone or alter the illness, but the reversal or removal of said illness is still wonderment.

It is my conclusion that God created an extremely complex mechanism called the human brain and all we know about it would fit on the head of a pin. It is my belief that God created it in that manner and intended it in order to keep things in order.

Dr. Samuel D. Wallace

Dr. Samuel D. Wallace added his signature
at the end of his channeled message

Adaline Hall
1854–1884

Chapter Nineteen

Hello, my name is Adaline Hall. Everyone called me Addie for short. I was born in Meigs County, Ohio in 1854 and never went very far from home as I just never needed to. I had two sisters, one older, one younger and two little brothers. My daddy was a Farrier and worked for a livery stable close to town and did most of the entire horse shoeing in that area. I was married to a boy named Mathew Hall when I was 17 years old. He was 24 and in many ways was still a boy. Although I was a very pretty young girl I was the most backward shy thing around. Mathew liked this thinking; he could control me and keep me in a place of submission as he liked. Things seem to repeat over and over throughout time as did in my case. It seems that Matthew was very much like his father and the way he treated me was much through the example shown by his father over the years. In their home it was accepted as a means of direction to hit a woman as long as the man's fist was not drawn closed and the blow was received below the face. So not until after we were married did he mention his method of direction and correction to any of the many short comings he saw in me, and as all corrections came below my face, the abuse went unnoticed. Since I was the one constantly offending him I was the one that needed the most direction and couldn't believe that I was as misled as I was. Even though my desire was to satisfy Matthew it was as if though I was continually letting him down.

His corrections started way soon after we set up our home. He worked as a laborer doing most any work that was available. He used to drink alcohol a lot and spent a large amount of his wages doing so. Only once did I question his dedication to his habit and after his "correction" I never wanted to question him again. On occasional visits with his parents I so desperately wanted to confide in his mother as to the abuse behind the doors of our home, but as I so wanted to find refuge with her and sought only answers to better myself, did I then recognize the very same look in her eyes that I noticed earlier in the form of my own reflection. At the same instance I felt she recognized within me her own struggle and we parted realizing each others terrible fate, yet never passed a word between us. I ended up pregnant with our first daughter when I was just 18 years old. It was at the times when all was still in the house and Matthew was out that I realized I too was only a child having a child and how unprepared I truly was for all of this. I felt that as Matthew would abuse me physically he would also add a mental aspect and I have heard that this behavior in some ways makes a man feel bigger or more powerful. As it continued he desired more and more to help him continue to feel better about himself. We had neighbors where we lived and on one occasion as friends were over and circumstances would have it I was found coming from around a building with a neighbor alone as Matthew was coming in our direction. It also added to my peril as I just happened to reach to flatten my apron at the very instance we were spotted. With a young baby, an abusive husband with needs that could never be met and I being 18 years old and very beautiful, I was labeled a harlot by my husband and accused of inappropriate, lewd behavior with my neighbor friend. That is when the mental antagonizing started to get worse. Through all of this I was ordered to give him another child, which I did. In his mind I guess it was my way of showing my faithfulness to him over and over again. I had another darling little girl and then two years later a little boy named Harlan.

    I did my best to cope for the 3 small ones and Matthew's drinking from the bottle and his controlling moods continued to get worse if you could imagine. His mental abuse and his constant belief that I was unfaithful to him and how I needed to keep giving him children or, "he'd smack them out of me" he'd say, it was very hard for me to accept. I then took the children and went to my parents' house, for the safety of us all is what I feared. But Matthew was allowed to come and in subtle ways just as hurtful and abusive as he had always been just not with his fists.

It was at this time in my life that I was feeling trapped and alone that I realized that the rest of my life was laid out before me and as much as I disliked it, there was not a thing I could do about it. I then had my mind behave as a child and I fell within myself and began to cry. I cried and shook and left my body as I no longer desired to continue with my destination. Matthew was nothing more than a drunk at this time and as my father was disabled on his back from an accident, mother and I were unable to care for my small litter. The children were sent to the home for children's care and I was sent to the Athens Lunatic Asylum in order to find a way to behave in a manner that would allow me to be with my children again. I was admitted in 1879 and was lost within the walls of an asylum. On numerous occasions Matthew would be found sober enough to come to visit. I believe deeply that it was not the desire to be with his wife or the heartfelt hope that improvements would be found within me, but rather the burning in his loins that drove him to visit. Each visit found him still abusive in his manners and any steps that would be made by me to help myself would be lost in an instant upon his visit. Perhaps his visits would be once every month or sometimes every other month.

It was the year of 1882 that I found myself with child again while still within the confines of the asylum. Of course Matthew accused me again of my unfaithfulness and it was the first time in my life that I honestly could not disagree as for this time I couldn't be sure as to whom the father was due to all of the other relations that were allowed to me. It was also this year that word came to me that Matthew was found along a road beaten to the extent that it was unlikely for life to continue. In ways you probably could not understand this word brought a great amount of relief to me and

I believed that my recovery and healing could then take place. In 1885 I gave birth to my fourth child, another baby girl. And just as I believed that I could now gain in my steps again I was knocked backwards as I was informed that I was unfit to be a mother and this little baby was to go away and I was to stay. I lost track of little Abby and I lost hope of ever feeling whole again. In 1884 I was given word by my father that my two girls were adopted and found new homes, but my little boy Harlan was still in their home. As I lay at night going over and over the details of my life and the reasons why, I continued to cry; not cry as you would for an expression of sadness, but as one with the deepest of hurts. Hurts that scar the very soul of a person and that is how I would cry.

    I put together a plan and decided that to continue on in this manner of minute by minute torture was proving to be most unfortunate. Although Matthew had been gone for over 2 years his words were in my head and his blows were still in my heart. So although he was no longer visiting me he was still very much within me. I found a rug near the halls of a wing that was braided of the most spectacular fabric, and as I had rehearsed in my mind many times before, I removed two rows of the outer braid. Only this time with my hands and as if carrying out a command that was not heard. I was able to fashion a most crude knot and loop that would allow me to hang by my neck until all of the putrid life that was within me would cease and that was the last of Adaline Hall. It sounds as if these accounts will be sought after from great distances and that a new understanding will occur as to the misconceptions of the Athens Asylum for the Lunatics.

Adaline Hall
1854-1884
#41

Mahala Butler
1842-1917

Chapter Twenty

My name is Mahala. I was born in 1842 in the state of Maryland, just outside of Cumberland in a small spot called Quincy. It really only amounted to about 7 families and a station or stop for early stages and such, but my parents were quite simple and liked to be by themselves. There were six children in my family and I was the 5th born child. My father worked mostly that I remember with his hands and he would contract with a few other men to hew railroad ties of white and red oaks and sell them for ties to the railroad. My father was quite the handy man with an axe.

When I was 15 I was set to marry and did so 2 days after I turned 16 years old. I married into the Butler's and married the wild Taylor, Thomas Taylor Butler. In the year 1858 times were hard not only in our valley but mostly everywhere. Work was hard to come by. The country was having awful pains about so many things. Negroes were a big talk and slaves running and being caught and just so much uproar it seemed at times that it was hard to go any place and sit to find solitude to last any amount of time. Tom would work and did so many things. His most handy thing to do was to butcher. He could skin and hang a hog or steer in a quarter the time that most men could do with help. He was quite talented in that way. Although he would work a lot it seemed that many folks were not willing to outright pay him for his work, but were always willing to share a slab or quarter for his efforts. Almost all of the time our smokehouse was plum full, it was hard to have any for flour or sugar or even fabric pieces. Tom had a way of trading the other way also. He would save up hams or bacon and take them to town and then trade backwards in order to get the simple supplies we would sometimes need. It seemed that everyone had something to give or to move in order to receive on the other end. In most ways it worked well and was a very effective way of making do.

In 1860 our first child was born and came out twice! I mean that two little boys came out looking exactly alike and behaving the same also. We named them Taylor and Jefferson. Both boys grew like weeds and were quite strong. When the war started, Tom stayed back not because he was afraid or such, but because of his responsibilities at home, but I believe more as to not quite knowing where he stood. He often said if a man is to get into a fight he'd better be damn sure what he is fighting for or for whom! I don't think we really understood what this war was really all about. It seemed that Tom was the only man for a hundred miles in most any direction so his butchering services were most useful.

In 1862 some men came around and put quite the pressure on Tom and off he went to do his part, which was a good thing for him as he went into the service of the North as a butcher. I was somewhat relieved as I felt he would be spared having to partake in the unpleasant life of a soldier. As much talk about fighting was abound it was agreed that I would take the boys and go west to Ohio to stay with cousins until this war was over and that is just what we did. I would receive somewhat regular letters from Tom as he would stay in place frequently. He would prepare meats in forts or large encampments, and as he explained, he would sometimes occasionally hear the sounds of war, but only at a great distance.

The war drug on from a small one year war to five years and it seemed as a lifetime was spent waiting for the return of my love. As Tom found our surroundings in Ohio quite favorable and the demand of his trade abundant near Chillicothe, we agreed to settle near town. With the arrival of my man soon to follow was a string of children as well. We had eight children all together and two of the little ones didn't make it to live long. The first died a few weeks old and as we never did determine why she did not survive, we treated her in the same manner as we knew how. But my last birth was the difficult one. I was 43 years old in 1885 and although I thought we would be done making little ones along came another. But sometimes looking back you wish you could do things different. But who's to know what lies before you and who gets to dictate the outcome?

This last little babe was born and the labor was long, very long and the baby was born blue and still. That again was very hard on me. Also it seemed there was a large amount of tearing with this one. Medically trained people were not abundant then and much was relied on midwives, and sometimes I wonder how much they actually knew about birthing. On our fourth child a section of the baby sack was allowed to stay inside me as it was overlooked. It started to fester and infect me from within with fever and other unmentionable occurrences. It almost took my life then as well.

But back to the last birth. The baby was born blue and cold and due to the damage caused in its delivery I bled and bled a lot. The midwife had only limited experience in this and packed my hole with cotton and tied a cloth around my knees. She tried black cohosh tea to try to provoke my uterus to clamp down and restrict my blood flow loss. She sent word for a doctor to visit. I lost large amounts of blood I was told. The doctor was more successful in slowing the flow. At times it would stop and I was quite weak, but a shift in my weight or position would start it along again.

As to not bore you with all of the details, what I was told happened was that in the days to follow my blood desperately tried to clot and heal itself; a clot got up into my heart and clogged up the route and caused considerable damage. It was through this clot that most all of my left side went numb. My arm would hang, my leg would drag and even my face seemed to sag. It also affected my brain as I had difficulties in speech, memory and somewhat basic skills. My left eye even behaved differently. I had a few nice people around me to help aid in my recovery. Although I bled for a long time I somehow made it through. Tom found it difficult to raise the children, provide for them and their needs, and tend to me and all of the special needs that I required.

We heard of The Athens Lunatic Asylum, but although we both knew I was not a lunatic we did know that (as we were told) it was a hospital of sorts and that they perhaps were better able to help me. We were also made to believe that many new treatments were spoken of that may aid in a mild if not full recovery. So in 1887 we went to experience this full recovery. Although Tom and the children visited as often as they could and even friends would visit, I was desperately lonely and wanted to be home. So after only four months I returned home to try to make it there again. Only four months of that and both Tom and I realized that the extent of my care was far greater than what was able to be allowed by Tom and friends. So back to Athens reluctantly I went and was once again admitted to the asylum. The care I received was not tender, but more routine if you may; wiping, feeding, dressing, bathing, directing, etc. The staff seemed to change quite regularly and so did the levels of care. You needed to know me and be around me for long spells in order to understand my unique speech pattern. So with each new staff member it seemed that nobody really got the chance or should I say "took" the opportunity to learn of my needs or requests. I was visited often by Tom and the children throughout the years and I was quite strong for being as invalid as I was. I moved about only at the pace of a snail, but regardless I would move about. I was quite taken by all of the people at the asylum and each with so many limitations. The care at the asylum was so different. It was at most times the extreme basics of care as there were so many patients and so few staff. For the most part I and we were on our own, only we were nonetheless limited within the confines of the walls.

My babies grew up and had babies and they would bring them to visit me. I was glad for that. Although I greatly disliked my circumstances I tried to exist and do my best. I was at the asylum for 30 years. It was a slow 30 years. I made basically no improvements other than I became quite strong in my good leg and good arm as they seemed to do the work of two. I did everything else at half the speed and found very little to pass my time. I never did learn to read and I could write only the very basics. I could not write letters nor could I receive them without the aid of a translator. I used to remember my fondness to whittle small flowers from twigs, but a pen knife in a lunatic asylum just wouldn't do! I found myself doing whatever would make the sun go down the fastest; from sorting laundry, to rolling bandage rolls or limited cleaning of the halls. I was lonely for 30 years and was overjoyed the day my body quit! My endurance for my pathway had been spent. My family and children mostly is the sole reason I lived to 76 years. Had it not been for their love and support my stay at the asylum would have been shortened dramatically without any doubt. The reason I was buried at the cemetery is due to the fact that all of the children were scattered and there was no real home place anymore nor was there any family cemetery. So as to my being there for so long, I guess it only made sense to stay and that is exactly what I did.

Mahala Butler
#398
1842-1917

Hampton Dixon
1859–1899

Chapter Twenty One

My name is Hampton Dixon. Lots of people call me "Hemp." Only a few tried to call me Dixie, but they were few since I'd most likely smash their face in if they tried, so they didn't. I had a rough life and it turned out that a lot of physical violence spilled over my growing up and into my adult years. I was born in Pennsylvania the oldest boy in a family of four boys and one girl.

My dad was a rough man and worked in the woods cutting timber like everyone else did as that's all there was. My dad went through the war and drank most of his waking hours. I know if he could have figured out a way to drink while he slept, he would have. After the war his head wasn't right and he was just plain mean. He was shot in the war in his left arm above the elbow and though the ball didn't hit his arm bone, it took a big chunk of muscle. His arm healed over and looked really bad without the muscle, but it didn't stop his ability to beat his children. He was mean all of the time. If he came out on the porch and saw a dog sleeping he would haul off and kick it for no reason even though it wasn't in his way. I saw him do senseless things like that often and you would think if someone enjoyed that he would have grinned or shown some sign of enjoyment, but not him, he had a pissed off look and a bad attitude all of the time.

When I was 14 I started cutting in the woods and my main job was to top the trees after they were cut. I liked this work and took any opportunity to learn to do the felling as that was easier work and more pay. So through much watching and listening I started dropping trees when I was 18. I liked the quiet solitude of the woods and it got me away from dad. Even though we were in the same wood lots I would often stay clear of him whenever I could.

My dad beat me and my brothers like he used to kick sleeping dogs, for no reason and for no visible enjoyment or fulfillment. The reason he would stop most times is because he would pass out. He would beat my mom too and had an entire life of meanness. I took the abuse because he was my dad and somehow I think I felt that since I was his kid it was allowable or something. I left home and lived with some friends when I was 18 and didn't realize until then that my view of people and my surroundings was quite twisted and I connected it all to the way I was raised and what I went through.

I recall being home when I was about 20 or 21 and I thought my dad knew not to try that crap with me anymore as I was 6 feet tall and weighed about 250 pounds, but as usual he was being his usual drunk and mouthy self, randomly throwing something or slapping someone, when he completely came unraveled on my little brother. I think something snapped in me as I saw my little brother getting hit on, and looking around, my mother did nothing and the others were afraid to do anything. I think as I remembered it was like watching a segment of my life and my little brother was just covering himself all helpless. I felt he desperately wanted someone to help him as I would if I were him, so I did.

I grabbed my dad by his hair with one hand and without a thought my other hand landed a blow to his face and blood went flying. I broke his nose and some teeth. As he bounced off the wall I noticed something snapped in me and I changed. I enjoyed being in control, being the one to come to my brother's rescue and all that. So I picked him up and beat him until two of my brothers pulled me away truly believing that I had killed him. I wasn't done yet - I wanted him to know what it felt like to be beaten. I wanted him to recover slowly, the same way we did. I wanted him to tremble when I came around as we did with him. I wanted him to experience everything he made us feel and I loved it.

Dad lived. But believe me he quit hitting my mom and brothers and sister after that because I made sure he knew I'd come back and kill him if he did. So here I was 22 years old, a big boy and stuffed full of all kinds of rage and resentment. I would snap in an instant and believed that talking something out was stupid and slow. All I'd have to do is beat the shit out of someone and I'd get my way and it felt good. In lots of ways I knew I was putting all of that built up anger in my fists and it came out on whoever crossed my path that day. It seemed I was always in trouble and fighting or healing constantly.

I loved to cut trees and was good at it; at least I thought I was. Maybe everyone was too scared to tell me I was lousy at it. I was always getting in trouble and I also noticed that it was getting harder and harder for me to stop. It became difficult for me to know when I should stop to avoid killing someone. The part that scared me was that I really didn't care. It was as if I became a different person when I would fight and later when I was told how badly I'd beaten someone; I really had no pity for them. That part always kind of bothered me, but it didn't stop me. Later I'd do the same thing and it would all just continue like a circle that spun around and around. Some people thought I should try to get help at a hospital and some just thought I should be shot to stop me. The bad part is that some men could blame this behavior on alcohol, but with me I never drank as I saw how it made my dad. Although I was just like him in his violence I never saw myself that way, but in many ways I guess I was worse.

I was 35 years old in 1894 and got word from this guy I knew that a small patch of land was going to be cut off. Work for a small crew of 5 or 6 was available, so I went as I was the head feller; the one that picked the timber and dropped it. This job was to take 6 months or more and I felt that if I would isolate myself I could maybe keep from spilling the brains out of someone. Well as my pattern of violence was just that, a pattern - I once again found myself beating someone for something trivial or perhaps very minor and this time the man died 3 or 4 days later. He just plain did not wake up. He had a smart mouth and was scrawny, but he was mostly a loud mouth pansy as I didn't thrash him that bad and he died. He should've kept his mouth shut to start.

After he died, I got myself put in jail and was held for his death. A judge and some others came and the fact that I acted like he deserved it and I wasn't sorrowful at all for him dying seemed to bother them some, I think. They kept me in that jail for about 4 weeks and wouldn't put anybody in the cell with me. Lots of people came to talk with me and tried to decide what to do with me.

Finally they felt I was not right in my head and that perhaps some good would come from my going to the asylum for the insane in Athens, Ohio. They sent me there and lots of people did a lot of talking so they placed me in the level with the same crazy kooks. I wondered, what was this all about? I wasn't loony like these guys I was housed with, I just had trouble controlling my temper. I had trouble with my head trying to make sense of just little things. The best way I can describe it is that I felt there is a certain pattern to your life; you sleep, eat, work, eat, sleep and that's about it, but for me it was all like scrambled up and made no sense most of the time. I didn't know when to eat and couldn't sleep. I got real frustrated when I just couldn't make sense of anything. They told me because I had killed someone and wasn't right, I would be here for a really long time, if not forever.

Well with that to look forward to I realized I wasn't going to get to have a woman and no children and no house and no job. All I had was crazy roommates forever! I stayed mixed up in my mind most of the time and nothing made any sense. I was confused when I was asked to do something like just go to my bunk. It didn't seem right or I didn't know why or something. I simply stopped moving as I didn't know what to do or how to do it.

One day the attendant that told me to move yelled it again really loud in my ear. Well that shook me for sure and I must have jumped a good foot up, but I still had all of this conflicting stuff in my head. What did not help is that he thought he would grab me by my hair and help me to my bunk. That didn't get him anywhere, because I snapped and turned on him and beat the shit out of him. Right in the middle of this he had help and there were two more on me and it was almost fun for me as they were hitting me with wooden clubs like, but I'd grab them and thrash them also. Two boys I beat really bad and the third one was about my size, but I think too much energy was used on the first two cause I just ran out of punch and that third boy was able to hit me with a club behind my knee and down I went. That is when about two more boys jumped me and got my best.

..."Right after that I was moved to what they called the cellar. This is the place they kept all the mean or violent crazies."

Right after that I was moved to what they called the cellar. This is the place they kept all the mean or violent crazies. They put me in this little room that had a wood frame for a straw filled mat and a bucket to crap in and that was it. This place was worse than the other. It was dark and damp; rats, spiders and centipedes were everywhere, but the worst was the crying, yelling, beatings and moans, almost all of the time. I could never escape these sounds.

Once a day a small door in the big door would open up and you were supposed to put your shit bucket out that door and if you did it right you could get an empty bucket and a plate of something they called "food." Sometimes someone would throw the shit out the door to make a point, but then no food would come to them and soon they would stop that. I'd hear stuff and sometimes guys would stop being fed because of this and would in some cases die.

I believed these nuts just couldn't understand. Life was harder for me as I would hear people moaning or talking and there was no way I could tell if it was in my head or in my ears. Once a week 3 men would open the door and come in with straw mats and clubs and told me to go to the back wall and strip naked. Then they would have me put a leather band on my ankle that had a rope attached to it that was held by a worker. I tried to tell them if they would leave me alone I would leave them alone, but it seemed they didn't hear me. They would lead me to a room that had buckets of water and soap and a drain in the floor. I was to clean myself up and if I got crazy and tried to leave or hurt someone, the one with the rope would yank me off my feet, and once down they would use the rest of the rope to tie me up.

I got to go outside about every 60 days, but when I went outside they had a rope on both feet. I only had a few problems after that but for the most part as long as they would leave me alone and not try to hit me then I wouldn't snap apart on them. This cellar was a very bad and lonely place. A large number of mistreatments took place and although a lot of the men there were really out of their minds, they still didn't deserve the treatments they received.

I ended up dying from moisture in my chest. I think it was because I was always cold or wet and couldn't dry out often. I died not many days after my birthday in 1899 and was buried at the asylum in grave #307.

Hampton Dixon
#307
1859-1899

Eliza Gerhart
1824-1880

Chapter Twenty Two

Hello my name is Eliza and these are the events that found me in the asylum for only 4 months. I was born in 1824. I was the 2nd girl of 3 and two brothers, both babes. My little sister Emma, I will mention later. I was born and raised all of my life in Washington County, Ohio near a small settlement of Swain.

The country at that time was new and so many changes were occurring. Advancements and discoveries were everywhere and you really saw things take off after the war ended. I was married to Daniel Gerhardt, a strapping lad with tan hair and big eyes as well as ambitions. Our country was being divided right in the middle and although there was no definite line of division, the separation was lying in each man's heart. How you viewed ideals, your convictions, who you stood with and to what loyalties you devoted home and line; the definite undetectable line of division. We joined the North. All of our family was here and we had no strong view points of slavery as we were not immediately involved in the containment of another human.

When the war was declared, my Daniel joined and left to aid in the cause, as did my two baby brothers, cousins, uncles etc. During the war times there were little boys, some really old men and the feeble were left to carry on the daily doings of the farms and settlements. If you were able and fit, you were without a doubt away fighting. So in our area there were lots of women and girls and a couple of handfuls of boys under age 11 at home. Those boys grew up fast though they had to.

Daniel and I had a small farm away from town about 40 acres with many essentials and means to survive. We had a great spring in these parts that was so well known, many would stop to water horses on their way to town. Daniel put a log trough near the lane so folks could stop without bothering to come to the house. We raised much of our food and were well settled. Daniel used to raise broomcorn to sell to a buyer of the tops and with 25 acres under corn we could do quite well.

Once the war began my sister Emma came to stay with me to help out, but mainly to be safer. Our mother passed away a few years back and that kept Emma at home often without anyone. So she came to me and we decided to ride the war out together. Things went smoothly for the most part the first year. Supplies in town were scarce; flour, fabric, oil, etc., but we did well to stay comfortable on our place.

In 1862 our world changed and not for the better. We received word that my brothers Edward and Edgar were both killed along with other family and friends. That was a very sad time for us and the reality of war sunk in. It was no longer some far distant story, but rather something we were now personally involved in, regardless of our feelings.

Then came September of 1862 when 6 men on horseback stopped for water. One came to the house while the rest stayed by the road. I knew by their looks and markings that they must be soldiers and was slow to come to the door. He asked for directions and asked other small questions that told me he was only fishing. I found it odd that he didn't seem to know that there weren't any men folk for many miles let alone here. I believed by the way they talked that they were some riders for the confederacy. The sound of their voices made me believe they were riding from the Southern States, although I saw no signs of allegiance to the South or the North.

Slowly all the men came into the side yard and plead for a meal and a bed in the barn. We had much of our supplies in storage and in hiding, but I believed that by refusing hospitality misfortune would soon rain down upon us, so a meal for six men was soon laid out before them. A small salt pork, boiled potatoes and a squash pie were on hand and they ate.

Our hope that they would leave us was shattered once a comfort was had and more questions were asked. Dusk found the men sharing a bottle and becoming more anxious and our company was requested in our front parlor. It seemed as soon as we stepped from the porch to the parlor the whiskey took effect and the true intentions of the men were known. We knew as much, but were slow to accept it. Emma and I had both had our men have us, so the act was not unknown, but the fact remained that none of the six of them were our men, nor were they invited.

Four men stayed on the porch while the lead man and another blocked our way out of the parlor and forced us to take off our clothing except for our petticoats (under gowns). They then forced themselves between our legs and took full advantage of us and that which belonged to our husbands. When they were finished, a call went out and two more came in and so on until all six men had their pleasures. When the last two were through the first two came back in and wanted to switch and this went on for hours and hours.

None of the men hit us, but they did violate our bodies in all manners known and often. After what seemed an eternity they tied us by the hands with the rope over the stair rail and left us in the front hall standing until morning. They jokingly said it was to help us drain! These men were vile and acted as pigs, so we viewed them as such. The next day they destroyed our home and piled anything of value into the front room while they left us hanging. I still had my under gown to cover myself, although Emma was completely nude.

This did not seem to stop them though as throughout the morning they would stop and randomly have their way with us, still hanging from the rail. We were finally loosened by the afternoon and kept in the parlor where we were allowed in a pot in the corner to relieve ourselves in view of watching men.

That evening two men rode in with two young girls. I knew them only as two young Henderson girls from a farm about 3 or 4 miles away. They were scared and looked to be about 15 and 16 to me. The day seemed to repeat itself, as Emma and I were made to prepare meals again, only this time we were not allowed clothing. We could only imagine what was being done to the two young girls by the sounds coming from the parlor while the meal was prepared. We watched the pigs gorge themselves on the food that Emma and I spat in only moments before. The second night was much like the first, only the rotation was not as steady as there were two more girls to be shared and the look on their faces was a look I would never forget. As for Emma and I, we had both experienced what a man wants and does, so it was not a surprise for us. For these two sisters all of this was new, painful and horrifying and I felt dreadful for them.

The next day found the men packing most, if not all of our stored supplies and after another round of abuse on their way leaving us with the feeling that they took such a great deal with them; all things that never belonged to them. The girls would hardly speak and Emma became obsessed with rinsing her mouth out as she had never experienced that with her husband. As for me, I only became increasingly mad.

We got the two girls back to their people and tried to get ourselves put together. We often talked about a plan to never be found helpless and in that position again. We were left with only knives for our defense as our guns were taken. I fashioned a small knife sheath which I tied sideways and kept on my front above my woman parts so that I would have full access to its handle if I was ever made to bend over and expose myself again in that position. Emma chose a small knife that she would keep in her boot and we placed all the knives and pointed articles throughout the house in many places we believed a man would try to take us.

Late November found two men again at our trough. The events seemed to repeat themselves as they had months before with the asking for kindness, food and other questions. This time I noticed a

CSA brand on their horse's flanks and knew they were scouts, spies or sympathizers. Events turned to a sexual talking again and this time they were bold and rough. We were both grabbed by the hair and led to different parts of the house. I was taken to the kitchen where I was forced over the table. The grip on my hair hurt, focusing both of my hands on his to loosen the grip and not on trying to stop what was destined to occur.

I was quickly shaken back to the plan that I rehearsed so many times over and over again in my head as my dress was raised, my woman parts were exposed and I was entered once again by a man unknown to me. When my attacker received his release his grip loosened enough that I lowered one hand to my waist and found the handle to my knife and at the very moment of his exit I spun around and pushed the knife to its hilt right above his hairline. The startled look commanded him to freeze and then just as I had rehearsed I quickly turned the knife over and raised my arm allowing a hole large enough to spill most of his guts on the floor. His cries went out as he fell and I knew his friend would follow soon so I waited behind the door. When his partner never came I moved slowly through the house without light until I found Emma sitting next to a man with her knife stuck in his neck. It seemed she acted quicker than I had as his trousers were still around his waist!

We dragged the bodies to a creek bed behind the barn and covered them with leaves and brush, but before covering my attacker I helped relieve him of his poker and balls and they would soon be eaten by critters of the woods! We took what seemed of value from the horses and hid them under the porch in a hole dug out separate from the cellar so that all of our supplies would not be discovered. Then we led the saddled horses a good mile from home and turned them loose.

My sister soon fell to the stress and became ill, but when Spring arrived, she seemed to have renewed strength. There were now 13 male bodies in various places around our farm. Most of them were in less than whole condition from when they arrived. Word came to us in 1863 that Emma's husband would be kept a prisoner and soon died as such. Then in 1864 my Daniel would stay forever in the state of Pennsylvania, never to return to me.

Throughout the war Emma and I continued to take travelers in the parlor and out to the draw behind the barns. We started to bury them when the stench reached all the way to the house sometimes and we needed to pick up parts out of the barnyard more than once due to dogs or coyotes leaving them behind. After the war ended, I found myself changed so dramatically from the woman I was that I rarely recognized myself in the mirror. Emma never had a man after that and found it difficult to be around a man at all. She became more and more withdrawn and behaved so oddly that I found it quite difficult to reach her on even on the simplest levels. I watched as my little sister moved inside of herself and became less aware of what was or could happen around her. She took less interest in bathing or dressing or keeping herself in an acceptable manner.

I felt that I had faired quite well through all of the events of the past five years most of the time. I was somewhat unaware that the urge to reach for my knife and push it into the head or loins of any man that came close had consumed me. The embarrassment of my assumptions led to fast and incoherent babble once he walked by. This only happened on occasion, but seemed to become more frequent. At first, I thought that the portrayal of an unstable woman was just an involuntary act meant to inspire pity in men instead of the dreadful sexual desires I seemed to attract to myself. I felt anxious, scared, my body often totally covered in sweat, my heart raced and my mind as if it would explode whenever one of these spells manifested.

Emma only stared into the distance and communicated less and less. Our experiences through the war brought about the defense of our very existence. We did what was necessary to survive and although there were many events that were not shared the impact upon each of us was felt in similar root ways, but surfaced differently. There was always the fear of being dropped in on at night and not being able to defend ourselves. Each encounter varied with the callers so the outcome did as well. Our goal was always the same, but the means to achieve this was always different. Sometimes it was necessary to surrender our bodies as much as we disliked the act of the violation in order to ensure the best possible outcome, and I believe that was very hard on Emma.

I would often find Emma in a dark part of our house sobbing for her husband Charles. He was a good man and I would hurt for her also. I remember the feelings that we shared of hopelessness and isolation. Tracks in the snow alerted us that our small cache of stored foods under the porch floorboards were discovered and completely emptied while Emma and I were to town. Events that you wouldn't even speak of or entertain for a moment in your imagination were often made reality for us. We ate horses. We would have eaten dogs if we had a means to shoot them. We ate cattails and wild foods and did whatever was necessary to live.

I walked to the drain and sat on the bank to observe how our callers were fairing sometimes and noticed how survival was impressed upon me in simple ways. I noticed that a dead man would swell to almost twice his normal size before he would split open, if I hadn't already done that and the worms would cover every inch of his body and crawl from every hole and in most cases create new holes. As I watched the busy worms moving and eating I believed they, too, were surviving and as unpleasant as it must have been for them to eat the rotted flesh of this pig of a man the task was accepted and completed efficiently in order to survive and a lesson was taught and a lesson was learned as to the unpleasantness of survival.

It was in 1867 that I traveled to Wisconsin to recruit the aid of our older sister, Elizabeth. She and her husband lived in the upper part of the settled state. Word was sent ahead and we soon found our sister and hoped to find help for Emma as her condition only seemed to slip deeper and deeper with each passing month. We took the rail to Cleveland, Ohio, then we'd take a ferry to the town of Milwaukee, Wisconsin and from there we would need to find some other means to a place called Madison and all three sisters would be together again.

Emma and I made it to Cleveland and even found the ferry and got to Milwaukee, but it was busy and trying to find transportation to Madison was very difficult. It seemed that very few knew of its whereabouts and even fewer were going that way and no one had room for two female travelers. We found ourselves waiting and sleeping in sheds and such. It was difficult to keep our appearances presentable especially with Emma, who plain didn't care. We had only enough coins for basic food and many times we discussed laying a trap as if we were spiders: offering to raise our dresses in exchange for coins and when finished, using our knives to relieve them of all of their coins! Desperation set in, my condition worsened and my social skills became more and more unpleasant.

While sleeping behind a dry good store, Emma and I were discovered by two men. We were awakened violently and forced to recline over boxes in an all too familiar position to be violated again. We were mostly exposed with our hands held waiting for the predictable event and our clothes were gone as well as our bags. Our coins and valuables were taken due to the commotion and we were discovered by a representative of the law. The men fled and we were left positioned so that anyone passing would have full view of all that was sacred to us and now of little value anymore.

We were taken to the jailhouse and found a place to sleep. Whenever I tried to communicate our plight and plans again the overlap of silly thoughts took over and the translation of our intentions was lost. Elizabeth could not be reached and we were both visited by the doctor and diagnosed to have lapses of mental distress. After nearly 3 months of confinement we were claimed by our sister and were released to her care. Elizabeth and her husband lost their home due to a fire, so they came back to live with us at our home in Swain.

We all lived on our little farm. Emma never seemed to improve, so we all cared for her as best as we could, and as for me things seemed to be up and down. I managed to function on fairly normal levels throughout the next 13 years. It became more and more difficult to care for Emma as she deteriorated so with the help of a doctor we decided it best to place her in a new hospital in Athens called the Asylum for the Insane. We were told that the sole reason for the hospital was to help care for those suffering the extended effects of the war and that the levels of care were far greater than anything we could provide. We took her there and were very impressed by its grandeur and knew that an acceptable decision had been made.

I came back home and did my best to cope and found that as I slipped away it seemed to take longer and longer for me to regain my composure. The world that seemed to be forced upon me was one of denial. I denied that anyone had ever violated my body or that I had ever killed men and discarded their bodies as garbage, even though my sister and husband found the bones of many. I denied the fact that my Daniel would never walk down our lane again although I had a piece of paper stating that he was not. I denied the fact that my mind was not acting as it should, even though I saw the frustration of those around me trying to help.

By the time I reached 56 years old, I was unable to communicate adequately and was consumed with the desire to be with my baby sister again. Plans were laid to take me to the asylum as well as we were all quite impressed with the care Emma was receiving and that is how I came to the asylum in 1880. My stay was quite uneventful. I saw Emma regularly and although it was a silent reunion, it still felt good just to be with her again. I stayed with two other women in a room at night and could come out and roam during the day. The food was only tolerable. The care was sustainable, but all was lacking. I never saw many men and only by the windows, but for this I was thankful. I never could sleep as the screams or moans always shook me into wide-eyed stares.

Then in November of my stay one woman jumped and swore I had eaten a piece of sugar candy belonging to her. I thought I was going insane, but I knew she was insane. She began slapping me and telling me to give it up or spit out. I had nothing to offer and tried to show her. The other woman joined in and soon as with packs of dogs, I was being attacked. I was overpowered and the choking I received ended my life and all of the remaining painful days I was certain to experience. I was glad to have it all end, but I was sad to leave Emma alone.

You are already aware that all of the people buried at the asylum are just that, people. Normal starting everyday people who tried to finish their experience and move on, but due to the horrific circumstances laid upon them they found it difficult to hang on and created an escape to a place less painful than the one that was directly in front of them. I was on earth for 56 years. I experienced much, I interacted and directed, I saw help, I touched and tasted, I felt, gave and received, I lived and produced, but most importantly, I survived.

Eliza Gerhart
#9
1824-1880

Elza (Francis) Stevens
1858-1896

Chapter Twenty Three

GREETINGS TO YOU, MY NAME IS Elza F. Stevens and this is my story. I lived with my mama, brothers and sisters and my daddy died from infection when I was about 10. He died and we didn't see him no more. That left mama to raise 5 kids and me, the oldest one, all on her own. We rented the back part of our house to a man or sometimes to a man and his wife. We always kept it for them to stay in so they could give mama some money to help pay for the bills. Sometimes they would help her around the house, but mostly they would give her money and all she had to do was add food to feed them. This was a help to her.

Mama showed me how to make rugs, so we made rag rugs to sell. We all worked at it, but me and my sister Janie were the very best braiders and we made them tight. The little ones ripped the fabric scraps we gathered and then others would stitch them end-to-end so Janie and me braided them and then rolled them into balls. Mama was good at stitching them and sometimes the people staying with us helped, but mostly it was just us.

It was told that I was born lacking and it was called Downs Syndrome, but mama said I was a good boy. I read and wrote a little but didn't like to. I liked to braid and work in the garden and fish, but didn't fish much. Mama started to cough and didn't quit until she died. The kids got to go to homes around uncles and friends, but I had to go to the asylum hospital. I was at the asylum and I liked it. I liked the people and they were good to me. I wasn't sick or nothing, but had to go where they could keep an eye on me. I told them I was a fisherman and a rug maker braider.

They let me braid in the Athens home, so I liked it. They had lots of fabric pieces in pretty colors. I made balls of braids big enough to sit on. At one time I had 22 balls in a shed and they found some girls to stitch them together and we made big rugs for people to buy with money. The girls didn't stitch tight like mama, but they still looked nice to me. I liked to walk on them with my bare feet on to help make them stay flat. I started in the middle and followed a braid around and around until I got to the edge then I turned around and went all the way back to the very middle. As long as you stayed in a row you couldn't get lost and I don't think I ever did.

I liked the Athens Asylum and the people. They were funny and made faces that made me laugh. Sometimes they ran outside with no clothes on at all - I mean nothing on but their skin. Then someone had to catch them and make them come in and try to put clothes back on. They were silly and funny too. Some men got food all over their faces or on their hair when they ate. It was a funny place to be.

The men with the keys took me to a building and let me make big balls of braid and I liked it and them. They were always nice to me and never yelled or nothing. I was fast and always made more braid than the girls made stitches. I got old and died at the home. I was sad to leave, but I had about 15 or 17 balls already rolled up when I died so the girls could keep on making rugs, but someone else would have to stomp them flat cause I went to heaven, so I couldn't do no more of that. Remember my name? It was Elza F. Stevens. My middle initial stood for Francis, my daddy's brother's name.

Elza Francis Stevens
#257
1858-1896

Charles Warrick
1874-1919

Chapter Twenty Four

My name is Charles and this is my story. I was born in 1874 in Springfield, Ohio and had an okay childhood. My dad and mom were poor and I was the third of four children. My dad and mom were born slaves and made it to Ohio after freedom was made available to them, so I was the first generation of black people to be born free in this country. Sometimes it seemed harder to be free. Meaning that when they were slaves they never went without food because the owner wouldn't want his help to starve or not be strong. Some food was always available and sometimes a house to live in, not very nice, but always a house of sorts. When you are free there ain't no one to ultimately fall back on and there ain't no food or house.

Free black people could get work most of the time, but the work was always hard and only jobs that the white folks didn't want were offered. Times were still hard on us even though my dad was free. My dad moved us to Nelsonville, Ohio where he found work. He found work as a tender that was for bricklayers. He would haul brick, mortar and water, everything but lay the brick. We called him a brick mule, 'cause all he did was haul things.

Dad did his best to keep us in school and wanted us to be educated so that we could use our minds, but when I was 13, I left my school to help my dad tend bricks. I got strong and fast and I had time to watch as the masons would lay brick after brick. I watched so closely and for so long until I decided I could do it and I tried. I was a natural at it; I was very good, fast and efficient and I could lay a straight wall with little help. I was moved along and able to become a mason. You had to take a test to become a full-fledged mason and part of the brick mason society and that kind of title wasn't offered to black folks in this part of the country.

I still wasn't allowed the pay, although I did the work equal to any white mason. I was an 18 year old who could read, write and lay almost 600 bricks a day and I got paid little more a black man hauling mortar. Sometimes I was sent off with a small group to repair jobs. I relined brick kilns or furnaces left from the war days, but I could fix bad spots with such a clean look, you had a hard time knowing the repair was ever made.

When I got to be 24 years old, I met a girl named Nancy who was new to our town and she and I hit it off. She was a round girl. She was not as black as me, but more brown and she was 4 yrs older. We got married. She was not that tall, but she was kinda wide. She was fun to ride, that's for sure, but boy, if you got her fired up, she could spit mad nails in your eyes. She liked to be my boss at home. When we was naked I'd ride her, but when we had our clothes on, she'd sure ride me!! She told me how much to do and for how long. She told me how much I didn't do and how long I ain't done it and she wouldn't stop. I mean she went on and on till I had to get away.

I started to need a place to go to get some peace and that is when I found that I could buy some peace and quiet in a bottle and the more I drank the more peaceful it got. I was 28 years old and drank most of the evening hours. My wife seemed to start to grow as soon as we got married and she started lookin' like her mamma. It was a slow thing, but it happened and didn't stop for a while. Like most men that got yelled at a lot and still getting a regular supply of pootie, I just didn't notice until one night I saw her across the room with no bed clothes on and that was the night I realized they couldn't make enough whiskey for me to accept all of this going on in my life. So I went to work and after I got my pay that day I left and didn't ever come back again.

I went back to familiar folks in Springfield, Ohio and found work there and never did tell nobody where I went. I imagine my wife kept on getting bigger and bigger until she just split open! I figured she went back to her people's house to live 'cause the shack we lived in wasn't that nice. I found a place to live and rented a room. I had my tools and continued to work with brick. I liked to escape at night with the drink and kept it up, so the rent for my room and board money was paid directly to them by my employer and everything, I mean everything else, I drank.

I had a hard time in those days 'cause my life seemed so useless. I worked hard with nothing to show for my efforts. I was 39 years old and rented a little room with a bed and a mirror. Due to being drunk all of the time, I kept losing my jobs and after so many in one area, nobody would take a chance on me and no work was to be had, neither was a room with a mirror, nor a drink. By the time I reached 40, I was suffering from severe depression and next to starving. I had nothing and no one and no place to go, but home.

I went back to Nelsonville and moved back in with my parents. My wife and her people moved away so I didn't have to deal with that, but I still had the taste for drink and it was strong. I lost my desire to be married all together, but now and then I would take a ride on a little black filly! Nothing more than a stick for them big draft girls brought back too many bad memories of my wife; memories I didn't want no more. They were always so quiet!

Dad found me work again and some men remembered my work and took me on, but just as soon as the money came in, so did my drinking and the circle started spinning again and again. I fell right back into being drunk, not able to work and being depressed because of all that, and my mind would start adding up all the good I'd done in my life and it wasn't very much. Dad couldn't stand to see me die slow, so he thought I would have a chance to be helped at the Athens Lunatic Asylum and got me a bed there. I had problems that I did need help with, although I wasn't really a lunatic or crazy man. It cost my dad and mom $5.00 a month to put me in there as they figured with my dad's pay that was all they could afford.

While I was at the asylum I had a rough time. My body went crazy without any whiskey and sometimes I was tied up to my bed to keep me from hurting myself. Those were hard times for me.

About a month and 10 days before I could think right again is when I realized where I was and what I had done to get put there and that it cost my folks to keep me here. I was in fact mostly a prisoner and could do very little to change anything about my circumstances. I slipped back into my depression and acted like a dead man with his eyes open.

I was in this condition more than any others, so the idea was to use therapy to shock me back into a normal person. Water therapy was used, but did very little to help and finally they used something called "jolt therapy" on me. They thought that by rattling my brain or making it jump, it would start to work again. I was led to a room where I was made to sit in a chair with my hands tied behind me and my feet tied to the chair and I had a cloth tied over my eyes. A man held a pole about 2 inches round and 2 feet long on my forehead while another man with a wooden hammer/sledge would strike the end of the pole. They had a rag pad on the end of this 2 inch pole to prevent it from being driven right through my skull. The chair was not bolted to the floor so that the impact would cause me to flip backward instead of snapping my neck. They believed that they could fix the damage or disconnect the front of my brain that was causing me to be depressed all the time.

With a sharp crack the pole sent me flying backward and my head hit the floor. I needed stitches on the back of my head and my brain swelled up and didn't go back down, so I never did function right again. Nine days later, I died and they actually sawed off the top of my head and looked inside to see the damage they did with the therapy. One more that didn't work. I was buried at the asylum since my dad had neither a place to bury me nor any money. Leaving me there was the cheapest thing to do. They did charge him one more month's dues for my headstone plus cost of burial and he paid it.

Charles Warrick
#612
1874-1919

Mathias Cook
1832–1907

Chapter Twenty Five

GREETINGS, MY NAME IS MATHIAS COOK and people called me Mathias for short. I was born in Germany in 1835 and came to the U.S. by way of ship with many other immigrants in 1852. I was 17 years old. I was trained to cut stone in Germany by some great stone masters. I was young, strong, eager, and active, but work was not plentiful as there were many workers and few jobs. A large amount of Germans left Germany in search of work and as new towns were developing all over the United States country many left for skilled work. The more skilled you were the better chance you had to find suitable work.

Being the oldest in my family it was time for me to move along and not depend on my parents and should the work I obtained pay well enough, perhaps I would have an opportunity to send money back home to help. I found work quite immediately upon landing in the United States. I was rapidly led to the quarries in Virginia and was cutting stones that were transported to the U.S. Capital in Washington.

I was a skilled cutter and knew stones and could see their grain. I knew the characteristics of each stone and could shape a stone with far less effort than those around me. I was moved up and around regularly. I was in Maryland, Pennsylvania and Ohio. I fell into the art of the arch quite by accident. I loved to build arches and found the work quite challenging, but more rewarding. I developed tricks and styles that were my own and was often made to oversee projects of great difficulty.

When I was beckoned between the Southern States and the Northern States I found myself in the midst of something I was required to participate in, but desired not to, as I understood neither its reasoning nor its benefits. Regardless, I was conscripted into the Northern army of the Potomac and was quickly assigned to an engineer's battalion. I felt that my skills would be of some use, but quickly learned that only my back was sought after by the army. My thick German accent as well as my sometimes-limited use of the English words made it difficult to convey my thoughts fully in adequate time and the uncovering of my stone abilities were slow to be noticed.

I mostly built bridges crossing rivers to allow armies and supplies to gain access to the side they did not already occupy. Only on one rare occasion was I allowed to repair a stone arch to allow transportation, but it was mostly the shoring up of the stone with timbers that was required and not the placement of the stone. It seemed that the majority of the work asked of me was timberwork was which was what kept me in the army and out of the line of fire and for that I was grateful.

Having completed my service I came home to Pennsylvania to marry my sweetheart and then moved to Dayton, Ohio. Not only was there word of work, but there was also a strong German influence in that area for which there was comfort through its familiarity. We had 4 children and lived well in this land, but as all good things tend to end, so did mine. In 1875 there was a large fire that consumed many buildings in Dayton. Many lost their homes and as well as their lives. This was the case for my wife, our four children and a big part of me.

I was in the Cincinnati area working on arched bridges and doing lock work and traveled home every two weeks, only now I had no home or family to travel to. In an instant my reasons for working to provide for my family as well as my desire was removed from me. My life and reasons for living changed in the small amount of time it took for me to read the news in a telegram. My family was all I had, all I wanted and all I cared for. The remains of my family were not found and I was left with only headstones and no graves to mourn over.

I found it difficult to mend the deep wounds that lay open and I believed time was healing my sorrow. I felt as if I would purposely keep the deep wounds open, as I didn't want to go on without their memory. I was the one responsible for the duration of the mending of my grief stricken heart. I never drank spirits as many do in times like this. A man generally turns to something that will result in a settling of emotions and allow the escape from the constant pain that haunts him, so I too followed this path. I found refuge and solace of mind in my work and I focused myself, my hands and my mind into my work for it was there that I could find my escape. I worked from before dawn well into the hours of evening and would take work of such difficult magnitude that there would be nothing left but my work and that was in fact my desire. I never again sought the comforts of the embrace of another woman as the thoughts of such were too painful and not allowed of me as I had one love and I sought not another. I made large amounts of money and achieved great accomplishments. I needed very little for my existence and found it only right to send the majority of my earnings home to the only family I had left. They still lived in Germany with the abundance and the brothers and sisters were able to all buy homes and even establish businesses in our homeland. One sister came to the U.S. and invested her money with her husband in the fabric industry.

I worked and lived and did very little else. As I became older my strength and sight left me, not all at once, but gradually and it was then I began teaching the finer aspects of the cutting and laying of stones. Eventually I was reduced to living as a boarder and as things would not be retained in my memory complications arose. Years passed and I fell to the frailty of my years. I needed to be cared for in more ways than would be expected by my boarding house. I was recommended to the asylum for the feeble in Athens. My stay was somewhat uneventful as my mind kept me quiet and inactive so the care needed to sustain me was limited. Gentle guidance for food and cleaning was all that was expected and offered. I saw many things at the asylum, but none that impacted me since my understanding had left me as well as the general use of my eyes.

In September of 1907 my body succumbed to the effects of general old age and dehydration, lack of good nourishment, inactivity and all things important to the vitality of life. I was chosen to add to this work by the group and agreed willingly! Interesting comment to note is that I am speaking mostly in German, my comfortable tongue. (Adem explained later that Mathias was speaking in German, but the vibrational levels received by Doug were translated into English!) Thank you for your caring work and as we will observe you will be richly rewarded.

Mathias Cook
#411
1832-1907

Simon Archer
1822-1890

Chapter Twenty Six

GREETINGS, MY NAME WAS SIMON ARCHER and this is my account. I lived an entire lifetime with not much of an impact, if you will. I lived low and quiet. I had some great children and a good wife, so those things I was most proud of. It was a tough time to live and make a living, but regardless of how tough times are, people still live, exist and carry on. My love was my family and the farm I lived in was my home place I bought from my parents when I was 28. My wife Elizabeth and I met when we were young and the two of us were foolish and I ended up under her skirt and put a baby in her. I got married at 23 years old and that's how that all happened. Once that pump was primed she started poppin' out babies one right after another. After three in a row she came down sick and took a spell to recover. Then she ended up having two babies born dead and we didn't believe she was able to go on. Then along came a baby girl and we had four. We lost one more after that and then due to the wrestling with her nerves she chose to lay with me only on certain days and no more babies came from that.

Farming was a good life for us. It was hard, but we raised most everything we needed. I got most of all of the equipment and stock when I bought the farm.

I was in the army in 1860 at 38 years old. I was already tired and stiff, but that wasn't sufficient reason to keep me out. I wasn't losing myself about this war. I would have been very content to stay at home, but things didn't seem to go the way I wanted them to. I joined the 78th Ohio Voluntary Infantry and was assigned to a supply attachment at the warehouse called The Wheel House/Cutwright Supply Corp.

I was assigned a wagon and a team and I was to move supplies from here to there, then from there to here, then from someplace else to someplace else and back again. I was told to get it there without losing my load. It didn't matter if I got myself killed, I was to deliver my load first and then I could die! My job was simple, yet important. I hauled whatever needed hauling; ammunition, food, bedding, beds, livestock, water, anything that boys living in the field might need. I wouldn't come home empty either. I hauled back caskets with poor boys going back home. I hauled loot or accrued goods. I never questioned my load, just moved it. I was always on the move and I was mostly behind our boys, so the idea of getting shot at wasn't much to think about. I stayed behind and supplied the big divisions and never went to the small outposts. I moved a lot of things over the years and got out without a scar or a medal.

I made it back to our farm and picked up where I left off; farming, the lack, rebuilding. We even tried the baby making part, but that didn't work out so much. We worked hard and we had enough food for our home, but little else. My oldest boy George died in that war. My boy Sylvanus and I took on extra work when we could. He hired on occasionally to a neighbor, Dave Munday, at his wood shop (Stock Chair Company). We did most anything; made rockers, benches, chairs, did repair work and even made caskets now and then. As I got along I started to develop some sickness in my chest. I coughed and had a hard time catching my breath and it seemed at times I wasn't getting enough air to live on. It wasn't but a year or two of this before I was told that I suffered from Tuberculosis or sickness in my lungs. I was around dust all of the time I thought triggered it and I figured just getting away from the dust would fix me back to health, but things were never just that simple. I was recommended to the Athens Hospital to recover. Although there was an asylum right next door, it was a good place to help recover. It took a great deal to get me to agree and as my condition was pretty far along, it ended up being just a place to die. The hospital was nice and we were asked to be outside most of the time to heal our lungs. We slept with the windows open even in the fall. The cold air risked making us real sick, but it seemed to help in the loosening of our chests. I was in the asylum for only a short spell when my lungs burst and I literally suffocated. They believed that the sickness would spread so I could neither have visitors nor could I be buried on my home place, so that is why I ended up at the Athens Asylum Cemetery. I liked the hospital, the people were kind and I was treated well, but not for very long. Again I say my life wasn't much to take notice of, but it filled a slot in the overall big picture I guess. Not all in these stories had problems with their heads, I was simply sick in my chest. Thank you for listening.

Simon Archer
#188
1822-1890

William Buchanan
1831–1891

Chapter Twenty Seven

My name is William Buchanan. I was born a slave in the commonwealth of Pennsylvania in the year of 1831. I lived what I believe to be a full and determined life. My life and events seem to be confused and overlapped with another Buchanan, a white male soldier. Although my father was white and a slave overseer, I nonetheless wondered at times when my mind was still, if I was half white and half black, why then was I not half free? Why? If I only retained half Negro blood, wouldn't that mean I was only half slave? Often answers never seemed to reach my questions.

I worked crops and livestock beef, poultry and some timber in Pennsylvania. I was never treated unjustly or brutally only what they considered fair. I was still another man's slave and that sort of life is never fair. My mother was born in Africa and brought here to be a slave and then died a slave. She was a beautiful, tall, fair skinned woman and was sought often for her beauty. She gave birth to 11 children, all different men, and I was one of those children. She never saw freedom in this land, but found it only after she died in 1857.

I was freed of my servitude in 1860, after much of what Abraham Lincoln was able to accomplish for the black people. The war began between the North and the South and although many freed blacks wanted to offer the needed assistance, even the Northern whites held back as putting a loaded musket into the hands of a black man still did not seem like a good thing for them. They were accepting support Negroes, little more than being a slave in a war. Although many were eager to lend support and to help the cause which would in turn free friends and relatives in the Southern states, very few were willing to tote or haul supplies as the desire to fight for freedom was stronger in us than was in most white soldiers. So reluctantly we held back.

Word came around that in fact the army of the North was indeed accepting Negro troops for fighting men. As the word went about the call for troops was heard and the response was accepted in great numbers. We met at Camp William Pen in Pennsylvania and received our formal training. We still were not given weapons of any kind and were forced to train with sticks and small strips of lumber. One reason was that there was simply a shortage of guns as all were needed on the front. Meaning that the country was still not ready to trust giving arms to a race of people that were beaten and enslaved for the last 100 years, and were in fact afraid that in doing so would be adding fuel to an already burning fire of frustration and resentment.

They had every reason to believe that as I, too, entertained thoughts of killing white men regardless of the uniform they wore. I was smart enough to know that should I find myself in a place where there were more grey uniforms than blue, then the odds of me returning to my former life would be largely increased. So it was only in our best interest to lessen the number of grey uniforms first.

I was given the rank of sergeant as I seemed to have a commanding quality about me and many simple minds seemed to respond to my organizing of them. I was in direct command of roughly 85 eager Negro soldiers. Although we trained for 2-3 months with nothing more than sticks and no uniforms. It was very soon that I was able to clean up these scattered men and had them all focused and working together. We were given uniforms from dead soldiers which were accepted at first for the need for warmth, but then through the persistence of our commanding officers we were given new uniforms. It was one more step toward the dignity given to a soldier. Still our skin was different, but out fighting spirit for freedom could not be matched.

Late in our training a load of used muskets were distributed, as well as sabers for officers. Many noticed that all arms given were used. When the sight of blood was noticed, the jubilation ceased and the reality of what lay before us became the reality at hand. We were shipped south to fight and did most of the sighting in of our weapons in two days. We were told that since we were black, we were better suited to the Southern heat and could fight better in that region. We were glad to be given the chance to be treated and seen as a serious fighting unit - The 8th United States Colored Troops. The rest in South Carolina was short-lived, but gave us enough time to collect ourselves and become stronger.

We were then shipped to Florida where we met our first Confederate Troops. It was not hard to fall into the grips of war as it usually only took one musket fired in your direction and the sound of that small piece of lead flying at you for you to realize that this was reality. You either stop the man shooting that lead or else he was going to keep going until he hit his target.

Fighting on sand was never pleasant. In fact doing most anything on sand was unpleasant since any time a bullet hit the sand near you, the small explosion caused sand to end up in your eyes. Battles in sand were some of the most miserable circumstances ever as sand was on and in every place in your body, and was in fact most unwelcome. Running or advancing was twice as hard as on dirt, but mostly there was little place to hide.

Our colored troops seemed to infuriate the Confederates as the thought of the Negroes shooting at them made us targets before most white soldiers. We established ourselves as a serious fighting force; quite impressive, sincere in our purpose and consisting of great valor. Our reputation grew before us.

Problems began with my general involvement in war and the sights, sounds and smells of battle on which I would not like to elaborate on too much. It was during a battle in Florida called The Battle of Olustee that my mind was impressed upon more than I would ever know. I was in command of 85 young men, all too eager to do what they had to and what I asked of them. We were asked to charge straight up the middle of the advancement against the already dug in Confederates. Reluctant at such a tactic, the white units were held back. I knew this was a suicide move, but many of the men behind me were unaware of the eminent dangers in what was being asked of them.

We charged at sunrise and were met with wave after wave of fire. Eventually the Confederates fell, but the 8th suffered such great losses in the aftermath that we were nothing more than a memory. As I retrieved the wounded, I could not help but notice the mortally fallen as their images would be forever imprinted in my mind. Knowing the outcome before my saber fell was the hardest thing I was ever asked to do and caused constant grief. The sights of the viciousness of battle and the utter barbaric nature of its course are ones that are forever left with a man.

We gained more numbers and went north for the freedom of all men and war never got any better. I was only slightly wounded on the surface many times and never realized the extent of the wounds I received on the inside until much later in my life. By the end of my service I was able to see Lee's army surrender; an event that was not soon forgotten. In a way I felt for the Southern men who fought with just as much determination as we did for a cause that they believed in as strongly as we opposed it. I was saddened in a strange sort of way that they never reached their goal or obtained the victory they sought. The conquering of a foe is never as grand of a spectacle as one would believe.

I came back to Pennsylvania to try to put myself and the country back together. I needed a new start and had the freedom to do so. I moved west to Ohio territory and resolved not to venture south. I was free to do so, but I felt it best to stay to the northern states. I took work as a farm laborer and did what I could to put the past behind me. I married a girl and started a family. We had twin boys, but one died shortly after birth. As much as I wanted to hide and take my life in a new direction, death followed me and the death of my baby son was overwhelming. I was visited at night by the ghosts of the men I sent so freely to their deaths; I so freely, and they so willingly. I tried to make sense of it, but never did.

They visited almost every night and although they never came right out and asked, I knew they wondered how I did such a thing knowing they would not survive. Were their lives not important enough to consider? Why was I not out in front if I believed in this action so much? Why? Why? Who was I that I was better and spared? What made this man more valuable that that one? What was the order to life and why was I given the authority to decide who should live and who should die? Was I God? Did I think I was? Who made me the one to decide? Could have refused my orders?

"...I tended to sleep mostly throughout the day and wander at night as my escape from the ghosts and treatments."

I could not go back now and change what had already happened. My life seemed to make little sense and have even less value. I was visited by the soldier's ghosts more frequently at night over the years. Since I avoided sleep when I had the choice, I slept off and on throughout the day and was thought of as a sluggard or a lazy nigger. I tried to keep to myself and failed as a laborer as well as a father and husband. It seemed I had failed even as a man. Eventually as my symptoms grew worse, I gave those around me no other choice but to admit me to an asylum for the mentally ill.

I was admitted in 1882 as a 51-year-old male and I lived under extreme conditions for 9 years. At first my wife and son visited me some, but due to their embarrassment that I was of unsound mind and my outward appearance, I was soon forgotten and left alone. I experienced the harsh treatments mentioned. Most veterans were exempt from such treatments, but I was still a "nigger" - deemed unequal to other men of lighter skin as was reflected in my treatment.

My symptoms grew worse in the environment. I tended to sleep mostly throughout the day and wander at night as my escape from the ghosts and treatments. Food, exercise and treatments were all but withheld from me. I needed to be awakened for feeding occasionally and began slowly wasting away. My guilt was overwhelming.

I found no relief until the day I passed and found peace beyond the separation for which forgiveness, love and equality were experienced. There is such hope available as a life that is unknown awaits us all; one of desire, joy and above all, freedom. True freedom that allows us access to the presence of God, our Father. An existence free from all of the burdens we possessed in life. I was a veteran, I was black, I was at the asylum in Athens, I was buried there, and I am free!

William Buchanan
#197
1831-1891

"...Perhaps the next time you cross paths with someone with mental illness, instead of pushing them into the corner, after reading this book you would in fact reach out with compassion."

Chapter Twenty Eight

So what do you do with this? You may do with it exactly what we did, nothing. Do not formulate an opinion or conclusion because you cannot. What happens in Athens stays in Athens! Meaning simply that what happens at asylums remains within the walls. Can we learn from this? We should! Do we? Not really. It happens and continues to this day. Why, you ask? Perhaps that mystery is something that needs to be solved as mental illness has been among us since the beginning of time. I do know this and feel that I can offer it without allowing too much: when an individual plans a life chart and includes mental illness, it is often more for the benefit of those around them than the one planning. Of course there is the other leg of this and choosing different directions at the forks in the path can often direct one to that scenario also. It is never black and white here. It is always continual shades of grey; dark grey to light grey and everything in between.

The stories have been told and have always been there, but often fade away as new events overlap each other and then become nothing more than part of the pile that no one desires to deal with. The asylum saw very large amounts of individuals with just as many differences in symptoms, as do all other asylums across the planet. Keeping all of this in mind, questions are created. I will verbalize only a few for you:

Is there much of a difference between today, tomorrow, yesterday and last year? Not really, especially when dealing with this particular subject. Very often people with mental illness are nothing more than a bothersome pain in the ass! Being different would in most cases continue on and not cause death, with the exception of a few. Accepting that fact, the vast range of symptoms would not lead to one's death. Being a drunk or a prostitute, talking to yourself, not sleeping at night, shaking or losing control of your bodily functions, getting old or being forgetful does not necessarily lead one to death. It does cause one to be uncomfortable around these individuals however, so away they go to a group setting so that as a group they would fit in and not stand out and be so shocking. So let's fix them, because according to our standards of behavior they are weird and undesirable.

Often we found that the cure could kill them and did. Does that mean we stopped trying? Look at today and allow the overlap of yesterday before you make a decision. Jolting a person to sense, shocking them or placing them in water are all torturous responses to the symptoms. But are they really? At the time of these events, we were learning and as clueless then as we are now as to what really causes this behavior. It is so very different from the simple treatment of a cough since mental illness manifests in so many different symptoms.

Today medication is still tried and a response is waited for. Should it cause convulsions, internal ulcers or harmful reactions, a different approach is then taken in the form of another drug that often only masks the symptoms and allows the individual to be still without really curing the malfunction. The mind is so vastly complicated, that only the surface of its potential is scratched. So there isn't really much of a difference from our procedures then to today. All were searching and trying, although today one's eyes do not pop out of their head, nor do they cook to death from scalding, or die from electric shock or pain, but heart failure, seizures, ruptures and convulsions, on the other hand, do still occur. Since it is mainly internally confined and not as radical, perhaps that means steps are being made in a positive direction or perhaps not.

Now that some of it has been laid out for you, what will you do, or better yet, what should you do with it? - Most likely nothing, to be honest. Neglect it and give it no conclusion. Leave your feeling toward it open, for if you recall; there is no black and white. Place it in a corner out of the way much as is done with those suffering with mental illness. They are placed out of sight and out of the way so that we do not have to form a conclusion or really make a decision either way. Perhaps the next time you cross paths with someone with mental illness, instead of pushing them into the corner, after reading this book you would in fact reach out with compassion and realize that under all that weird behavior is the same person that is reaching out, yes, you. Only they, too, are reaching out in a different direction. Consider all of this as a whole and be very slow to draw conclusions as the lines of definition are continually in motion. It has been my pleasure.

Red

OFFICIAL NAMES OF THE ATHENS LUNATIC ASYLUM

1874-1911: Athens Lunatic Asylum

1911-1944: Athens Asylum for the Insane

1944-1968: Athens State Hospital

1968-1969: Southeastern Ohio Mental Health Center

1969-1975: Athens Mental Health Center

1975-1980: Southeastern Ohio Mental Health and Retardation Center

1980-1981: Athens Mental Health and Developmental Center

1981-1991: Athens Mental Health Center

1991-: The Ridges

Acknowledgments

Research/Archives	Doug McCabe
Book Title	Bryan David DeLae
Book Cover	Balboa Press
Spine	Balboa Press
Photos	Bryan David DeLae
Photos	Brigette O'Rourke
Photos	Danielle Russell
Photos	Tom Miller
Photos	Reyna Garcia
Editing	Susane Martinez
Technical Assistance	Bonnie Parham
Personal Assistance	Danielle Russell
Writing consultant and support	Sharon Grossman

Official Names of the Athens Lunatic Asylum and many other resources: Courtesy of Doug McCabe / Curator of Manuscripts, Mahn Center for Archives and Special Collections, Alden Library, Ohio University.

Special thanks to the Athens Historical Society and The Robert E. and Jean R. Mahn Center for Archives and Special Collections, Alden Library, Ohio University for their extensive collection that was made available to us for our research.

We also wish to thank the Ohio University Legal Affairs Department, for their assistance.

A warm thank you to Doug and Valaria McCabe for graciously giving us a place of solitude where we could focus and finish this manuscript.

Thanks to the Balboa Press Team for their assistance.

Our deepest appreciation to Lavelle and Associates for their legal assistance.

CPSIA information can be obtained at www.ICGtesting.com
Printed in the USA
BVOW02s1707230813

329255BV00001B/4/P

9 781452 571836